"We can all look at the statistics ____ ____ __ ____ ____ many who are raised in Christian homes and churches are leaving the faith when they graduate from high school. We are experiencing an epidemic of loss within the Christian community. Jim and his dad, Bill, have mingled practical principles with true life stories to form a helpful guide for both keeping kids from becoming prodigals and winning them back once they choose to run from Christ and His church. This book is helpful for individual parents and for churches that experience the loss of those they helped to raise in the faith. It will give you hope as well as clear steps to do your part as a parent and church member."

—**Josh McDowell**, bestselling author,
Evidence That Demands a Verdict

"*Hope for the Prodigal* is raw, vulnerable, and incredibly helpful. It's a practical and powerful look into the heart and response that God has toward His own prodigals— and the kind of heart and response He calls us to have toward the prodigals in our own lives. It will leave you encouraged and better prepared to participate in the greatest of all miracles: the restoration that flows out of genuine repentance and forgiveness."

—**Larry Osborne**, pastor, North Coast Church, Vista, CA;
author, *Thriving in Babylon*

"Every now and again God gives certain people a heightened understanding of what He is all about and what He wants us to know about living an abundant life. Consistently, God has chosen my good friend Jim Putman to deliver an important message that touches so many people. *Hope for the Prodigal* is important because many of us have strayed or know of someone who has strayed into a dark and dangerous place and we want to know if there is a way back. Jim, with the truth of God's Word as his guide, leads us step by step back into a place of rich inheritance and blessing. Whether you are the prodigal or it is someone you deeply love, Jim reminds us that the story isn't over yet. Read this great book and find your way back home."

—**Randy Frazee**, senior minister, Oak Hills Church, San Antonio, TX; author, *The Heart of the Story*

HOPE
FOR THE
PRODIGAL

HOPE
FOR THE
PRODIGAL

Bringing the Lost, Wandering,
and Rebellious Home

Jim Putman *with* Bill Putman

BakerBooks

a division of Baker Publishing Group
Grand Rapids, Michigan

© 2017 by Jim Putman and Bill Putman

Published by Baker Books
a division of Baker Publishing Group
P.O. Box 6287, Grand Rapids, MI 49516-6287
www.bakerbooks.com

Printed in the United States of America

Library of Congress Cataloging-in-Publication Data

ISBN 978-0-8010-1908-1

Some names and details have been changed to protect the privacy of the individuals involved.

The author is represented by WordServe Literary Group. (www.wordserveliterary.com)

17   18   19   20   21   22   23   7   6   5   4   3   2   1

CONTENTS

Contents

Part 3: The NEW DEAL

ACKNOWLEDGMENTS

Huge thanks go to our church family, staff, and elders of Real Life Ministries, to Lori and Bobbi, all our children and grandchildren, and all our family and friends, to agent Greg Johnson of the WordServe Literary Group, our writing partner Marcus Brotherton, and Brian Thomasson and the team at Baker Publishing Group.

INTRODUCTION

The Story of Three Sons

It all starts with a story about *three* sons.

Yes, three. But in Luke 15, the biblical account of the prodigal, we see a father who had *two* sons. So where does the third son come into play? And what does this have to do with us and what we're going through? Chances are good you've heard the story. Here's a paraphrase to refresh your memory.

A wealthy father had two sons who looked and acted quite differently from each other. The older boy was considered the "good" son. The younger boy was considered the "not-so-good" son. One day the younger son said to his dad, "I'm tired of waiting for you to die so I can get my inheritance, I want what will be mine, and I want it now. Give me all I've got coming to me!" What an insult. In that culture, a son received an inheritance only after a parent had died, or at the earliest when a father could no longer manage his estate. For the younger son to demand his inheritance up front was the same as saying, "I wish you would drop dead, Dad. Get out of my way, Dad." It was deeply hurtful.

But the father was both strong and loving. He said something like, "Okay, son, if that's how you feel. If you really want what you think you want, then you can have it, but I know it won't make you happy." So the father gave the younger son what he asked for.

It didn't take long for the younger son to leave. He high-tailed it out of his father's house and headed for the ancient equivalent of Las Vegas. He was hell-bent on going far away from home. The money burned a hole in his pocket, and as soon as he reached that faraway country, he spent all he had on wild living. His money vanished like morning dew on a hot summer's day. In no time at all, he was broke. Dead broke. But he hadn't reached rock bottom yet.

Right about then, the young man's stomach began to rumble. Oops. He'd forgotten to save money to eat. None of his friends seemed to have any extra food to spare, or if they did, they were not willing to share. To make matters more complicated, a famine hit that faraway land. Jobs grew scarcer. People grew hungrier. Eventually the younger son took the only job he could find: tending pigs. In that culture, tending pigs was the lowest of the low. Even today pigs cannot be found in Israel. They are considered filthy animals that a Jew won't touch. But even that job was a bust. The young man grew so hungry, he found himself seriously considering eating the pigs' food. Picture that scene. There was the rich man's son who at one time had lived in luxury, now in the muck and mire, starving, miserable, broke, desolate, friendless, thinking about wrestling food away from pigs. That's rock bottom. But in that horrible and desperate and pressure-filled place, a marvelous thing happened.

The younger son came to his senses.

The son remembered life back home. His father lived well. His older brother lived well. Even his father's servants lived well. He'd been such a fool! "I'm starving, but there's plenty of food back at my father's house," he reasoned. "I should just go back home. But because of all I've done I don't deserve to be one of the family again. I'm no longer worthy to be a son. Maybe I can get a job as one of Dad's servants." So home he went.

The good father had continued his daily routine but always with an eye on the road, his hand shading his brow—watching, waiting, hoping. While the son was still far away, the father spotted him. Even though his son had left with riches and health, the father recognized him in rags, nothing but skin and bone, and the father sprinted down the road with arms open wide. He plowed into his son, hugged him close, and wept for joy.

"Welcome home, son," the good father said.

"I don't deserve to come home," the son answered. "I've messed up too much. I've hurt you too much. I'm no longer worthy to be called your son."

"Are you kidding me?" the father said. "You're my son no matter what. I lost you and now you are found—you were dead but you are alive again." He turned to his servants and said, "Quick. It's party time. Get the boy cleaned up and dressed in my best suit. Whip up a barbecue that'll make all the neighbors envious. Let's feast and celebrate, for my son was lost. But now he's found."

The servants cooked up the best kind of party. A true celebration. Great music sounded from every room. Family members and guests danced and feasted on the best food in all the land.

Meanwhile the oldest boy, the "good" son, was still out in the fields. Working hard like he always did. He heard the music and caught a whiff of barbecue and called one of the servants over to explain what was going on.

"Your brother's come home," the servant said. "All safe and sound. C'mon inside and join the celebration!"

"That betrayer?" said the older son. "You are actually celebrating his return?" The older son was furious and refused to join the party. He huffed and went back to work.

Back at the house, the father heard of his older son's behavior, so the father excused himself, walked out to the fields, and tried to coax the son to welcome his brother home.

"No way!" snapped the son. "That worthless excuse for a son brought chaos into our home. He hurt us all. I've never strayed from the path. If anyone should be given a party it's me! All I do is work, never complaining, never once disobeying you. But you've never even given me a small platter of steaks so I could celebrate with my friends. Then, when this other son comes home after spending all our money on wild living and women of ill repute, you throw him the biggest party we've ever seen."

"Hold on a moment," the father said quietly. "You're forgetting something very important."

The older brother was so angry he couldn't look his father in the eye. A few moments of silence passed, then he said, "What?"

"Everything I have is already yours. But we must celebrate—your brother was dead and is alive again—he was lost and is found. He is not just my son—he's your brother."

Is There Any Solution for Prodigals?

Three sons, remember? The older son who stayed home but nursed a bad heart; and the younger son, the prodigal who took his bad heart to a distant land—that's two. So, who is the third son in the story?

The third son is the narrator of this story.

Jesus, the *Son* of God.

The story of the prodigal son is ultimately a story of Jesus telling people about His Father. Picture the larger context. Jesus was telling this story to two groups: first, to teachers of the law, who'd been chastising Him for associating with "sinful" people; and second, to His own disciples—the young disciples He was helping to grow up in the faith. Jesus, the Son of God, wanted both groups to know more about what His Father is like. Jesus was telling them that His Father is filled with compassion, holiness, justice, and most importantly love.

The parable was multifaceted. Jesus wanted His listeners to know that He too loves prodigals—people such as the younger son. Jesus as Savior, just like the heavenly Father, never turns His back on the lost. Even when people are far from Him, squandering all their gifts on wild living, the Father is always watching, waiting, anticipating their return.

Throughout history God the Father has done more than just wait at the house for prodigals to return. He had sent messengers (the prophets) to say, "Come home." He had allowed circumstances to cause His children to think about coming home (such as famines that would get their attention). And He had finally sent His own Son to deliver the ultimate message—"My Father says, 'Come home.'" When sinners finally turn back, the Father runs to them. He embraces them, rejoices over their repentance, welcomes them home with arms open wide.

The parable also shows God's love for people who never flagrantly and outwardly disobey him—people such as the older son. Jesus wants them to realize that their works do not earn His love and that their hearts matter just as much as actions. This includes religious people, Christians, people who work hard on behalf of their Father, people who keep their noses clean. Jesus wants them to know that even if they keep their religious commitments, they can still be far away from God if they harbor bitterness, jealousy, anger, or lack of forgiveness. He wants them to realize how much the Father cares for all people—even prodigals—and how closely He values all His children. All He has is theirs.

Hope for Prodigals' Return

We have all been prodigals to one degree or another. This is a book about caring for them. It's a book of big hope. I (Jim) was once a prodigal. I was raised in a Christian home. My parents were both believers. But I strayed far from the faith as a high school and college student. I eventually declared I didn't believe anymore.

My dad, Bill Putman, was a prodigal too when he was a young man—not so much out of rebellion, like me, but out of hurt. Together we talked our way through each chapter of this book before the writing process began. He'll be sharing more of his stories and insights throughout this book, as well as adding helpful sidebars. As a young man, my dad came back to the Lord in a mighty way, and today my dad is one of my closest friends. He and my mom, Bobbi, are on staff with me at Real Life Ministries in Post Falls, Idaho.

One of my three sons, Christian, has also been a prodigal. Christian grew up in a home where both parents love and serve God. But Christian strayed from the faith as a high school student and young adult. He got involved with drugs and alcohol and had a baby out of wedlock. He's been to rehab twice and has spent time in jail and in a homeless shelter. But today Christian is back on track, walking with the Lord and serving as a youth minister.

In my life, my dad's life, and my son's life, a big common denominator was the prayerful role of other Christians (both our physical and spiritual families). God used other people to win all three of us back. The example and influence of others, as well as the Word of God and the Spirit of God, helped disciple the three of us back into real relationships with Jesus, and we are all actively serving the Lord today.

There is hope.

We invite you along on this good journey.

Jim Putman
Bill Putman

1

Broken Families, Broken Churches

*Two parents. Two different families. Two
different times of life. Two big stories of crisis.*

I (Jim) actually punched my son in the face. I hit him and knocked him out cold. He'd been giving my wife, Lori, and me trouble for so many years. We'd tried everything. He was angry, sarcastic, mean, critical, and rude. Not to mention he was into drugs, sleeping with girl after girl, drinking heavily, failing in school, and generally all-around defiant.

When he came home high and started bad-mouthing his mother, I'd had enough. I was furious. He called his mom some unmentionable names, and I just snapped. For the first time in twenty-plus years, I hit a man in anger—I punched my own son and actually knocked him out. The son I had fallen in love with at birth, protected, taught to play baseball in the backyard, and to wrestle; I had taught to know Jesus, had high hopes for—this son I had just punched in anger. How could this happen?

Our family was a mess. My wife, Lori, and I could not get on the same page about how to handle it, but we both agreed the way I had just reacted wasn't right.

Oh, and to top it off—I was a pastor.

What were we going to do?

I (Bill) was ready to leave my marriage, family, and ministry.

My wife, Bobbi, and I were hopelessly in debt, the total bill upwards of $96,000. Our daughter was pregnant at age fourteen. My oldest son, Jim, was an angry alcoholic. Bobbi and I were struggling in our marriage, just going through the motions, hoping to stay afloat. We didn't have answers for ourselves, much less for anyone else. The rebellion of our five children had sunk us into a crushing despair. For all our great efforts in life, our family was a mess. We had broken hearts and we were a broken family.

Oh, and to top it off—I was a pastor too.

What were we going to do?

Welcome to the World of Prodigal Care

Maybe you can really relate to one or both of those stories right now in your life. Your family is in crisis, maybe because of a prodigal child or a prodigal spouse. Or maybe you simply know someone who's going through a really rough time. This person may be in your extended family, your neighborhood, or your church. You care and want to help.

Welcome to the world of caring for prodigals. This book is for you.

It's no secret that we've got a prodigal problem in the Western world today. In the United States alone, research shows that the number of people claiming to be Christians is dropping, while the number of people who don't identify with any religion is growing.[1] Today, more than one in three millennials don't affiliate with any religion at all.[2] And some three out of four teens who currently attend church will soon drop out[3]—a statistic with a twist, which we'll tell you about in a moment.

I (Jim) have been a pastor for about three decades, my dad Bill for over fifty years, and we regularly meet with families whose kids have walked away from the faith. They've lost their kids to a culture that tells them the Bible isn't true. The media either attacks our concept of God or seeks to make Jesus only one of many ways to get to heaven. The culture undermines the biblical view of family and pushes kids into believing that Christians, churches, and the Bible are sources of bigotry and intolerance instead of the opposite. Most churches and Christian families have not done an adequate job of preparing kids for the assault on their faith.

Recently I had to tell some parents that they were making a huge mistake. They had missed church for a better part of two years, following their kids to every soccer game and tournament in the region. All for the hope of scholarships. They were losing in two ways. First, their children would need good spiritual friends to help keep them connected to Jesus in the future, but because of involvement in other things, their children had no real friendships in youth group and church. I told these parents that their kids needed to be taught about Jesus so they could answer the hard questions, but because they were not in places where spiritual truth could be learned, their kids were ill prepared. Making matters worse, spare time at home was spent working on soccer in the backyard rather than talking about spiritual things. Second, if their kids did get scholarships, the college they were aiming for likely would do its best to indoctrinate them in ideas such as the theory of evolution and the concepts of pluralism, so-called diversity, and tolerance, and would surround them with peers having completely different lifestyles and philosophies. I told these parents they were working hard to hand their kids over to a college and society that would likely destroy in them the godly values they said they cared most about. I told them that if they didn't change their priorities, they would one day hear things coming from their children's mouths that would break their hearts. How do I know this? Because I see it all the time. Because it is the story I see all around me now from others who traveled the same road.

I am constantly approached by parents who believe their children once walked with the Lord but are now apathetic or antagonistic toward Christianity. For many, their kids are now actively addicted to drugs or alcohol, or engaged in wild living, and the parents don't know what to do. Their hearts are broken, and they need encouragement and counsel. The unresolved crisis with their prodigal puts stress on the marriage, the other children, finances, and emotional health. They live on the edge as a result of the pressure and the cost of trying to save their kids.

How Can the Family of God Help Parents of Prodigals?

I believe there is much a church can do to help. Prodigals can be won to Jesus or back to faith! But too many churches fail to address the real issues and often make them worse by saying nothing or by saying the wrong things. Many parents feel bad, as if the failure of their children is all their fault. "If we had raised them right, then this wouldn't have happened," parents lament. Parents feel hopeless, fearing the situation with their prodigal children will never change.

There are no perfect human parents, so of course we make mistakes. We may need to make some things right, but blaming ourselves alone isn't going to fix the problem. Parents and churches can play a positive role in helping our prodigals come to their senses. Even if we do our part perfectly, it does not guarantee that they will choose to come home. But with our Father's help, we can play a strong part in opening the door to this possibility.

Will the Real Prodigal Please Stand Up?

What exactly is a prodigal? Often when we define the word *prodigal*, we use it only in the context of kids whose parents raised them in the Christian faith, but then the kids went off the rails and walked away from Christ outwardly and dramatically. That's definitely one picture of a prodigal, but to truly define a prodigal, we must broaden the definition.

A prodigal may be a Christian who once got saved but then drifted away from the Lord and no longer claims to follow Jesus. In other words, they are no longer saved. In my mind, the story of the prodigal son itself tells us that is possible. Now, I understand that this view may be controversial depending on your theological bent. There are a few ways we could look at this. Scripture tells us that not everyone who says "Lord, Lord" is really known by the Father, but only those who do the Father's will (Matt. 7:21–23). So it's possible that a person who is far from the faith but once claimed the faith never really had it to begin with. On the other hand, many seem to have a true conversion experience, begin to follow Christ, then walk away. God has chosen us and wants a relationship with us and will never change His mind. But some believe that a professing Christian can drift from the faith so far that they eventually give up their faith. Whether or not that person loses their salvation has been the subject of debate for a long time. Honestly there are Scripture passages on both sides of this argument. Either way, Jesus tells us we can know a tree by its fruit.

First John 3:9 tells us that no one born of God continues in sin. This does not mean that a Christian doesn't sin, because John also tells us that if we claim to be without sin we are liars. It means that a born-again person doesn't continually, habitually sin, or better said, they don't make a practice of sin. I once wanted to be a great wrestler, so I practiced wrestling in order to be good at it. I loved it. This vividly illustrates a person who is practicing sin. They love it and practice it as much as they can because they want to get good at it. A believer who has Jesus living within cannot love sin and want to practice it. When they sin, it doesn't feel right. They respond with something like, "Man, I can't believe I did that again." They feel inner turmoil as the Holy Spirit does His work. It may take a while, but they come to the Lord for forgiveness. John said that if we confess our sin, He is faithful and just to forgive us of all unrighteousness.

Many parents don't think of their child as a prodigal—spiritually lost—because this child once said the sinner's prayer. The parents may admit the child has slipped into a sinful lifestyle, but they are not concerned about their child's salvation because the child once spoke the correct words. But they admit that no fruit can be seen in their child's life. That's a red flag. Better to assume they need salvation. A parent will not rush to save a child in the river if they don't think the child is in danger, and a parent with no concern about their child's salvation does not seriously pray.

I am dealing with a man who once led worship in a church and later went to college to become a science teacher. Along the way, he began to have questions about his faith, and because he was busy and enjoying life, he didn't make time to talk about them. At the same time, those who were supposed to spiritually shepherd him didn't notice his absence or seek him out. He says that he eventually gave up his faith and now claims he is an atheist. He has a nice wife and two beautiful children. He has a moral set of values that looks Christian because he says that morals evolved to protect the species. He does not drink or cheat on his wife or get angry and say harsh things. However, he is a prodigal because he has no faith in Jesus; in fact, he believes Jesus was just a good teacher. This prodigal is no longer or maybe never was connected to the Lord or the family of God and is walking in a lifestyle and embracing heart attitudes that are inconsistent with the teachings of Jesus Christ. In this case, the relationship with the person's parents is not broken, but the issue is a broken relationship with the Lord. Fifty years ago we might have called this person a "backslider," although we don't use that term much today. This person is a prodigal who has turned away from the Lord and from the Lord's family, the church, and when we use this broader definition, more people can be defined as prodigal. It's not just a parenting issue, it's an issue for all believers. Thus many more people have an interest in helping prodigals find their way back to God.

We tend to view prodigals as addicts or rebels. But in this broader view, the prodigal can be clean and sober, succeeding at many areas of life. The prodigal might be married, educated, hold a good job, have kind and smart children, and be an all-around upstanding citizen. Parents may say, "Oh yes, Johnny is doing really well. He graduated from university and married his college sweetheart. He's working hard as a lawyer. They own a big house in the suburbs. I'm not worried about him at all."

Do you see the problem? Because the child is doing so well by the world's standards, the parents don't define their child as a prodigal. But we must use a definition that's measured by biblical standards. Teenagers from Christian homes who do drugs are not the only prodigals. A prodigal could be a good citizen. A family man. A member of the PTA. Someone living the American Dream. A church leader. The biblical standard is that if he's far from Jesus, then he's a prodigal.

An additional subset of prodigals aren't typically acknowledged as prodigals because they're still active in the church. They might call themselves Christians, be casual or active church attenders, pour their lives into ministries, and consistently work hard at doing right. They may have all the right answers when people question their beliefs, but they don't have a relationship with Jesus that is vibrant and growing. They have little real love for other believers. They're mired in anger, jealousy, bitterness, greed, lust, unforgiveness, or other sins. They may believe that being faithful means working hard and looking like a good Christian outwardly. But that person is a prodigal.

Remember, there are three sons in the biblical account of the prodigal son. The "good" son was just as far from his father as the son who left home. The older son undoubtedly looked good in society. But he didn't have a heart for God. He actually told his father he'd slaved for him for years. He didn't see his service as a response to the father's love but saw himself as a slave. He didn't understand the father's heart. He didn't understand the relationship he was invited to have with the father. Also, he didn't love or forgive his brother. He was bitter and angry and fuming and frustrated. He was just as much a prodigal as his brother.

So, based on the biblical pictures of a prodigal, we need to use a broader definition of the word:

> Anyone who has known God or appeared to know Him but who is now not walking with God is a *prodigal*.

We might say it this way: an unsaved prodigal is part of the human family and has wandered away from their Creator; a saved prodigal is part of the family of God and has wandered away from their Father.

Picture it this way: there are outward, public prodigals and inward, private prodigals. Outward prodigals are living in defiance. They might be teens or adults, have Christian parents or not. They outwardly defy Jesus Christ and reject His church. Inward prodigals, likewise, might be from any age group or background. They try to look good on the outside but are inwardly defiant to Jesus Christ, their parents, and His church. The difference is that often outward prodigals aren't found at church, while many inward prodigals are still there, going through the motions. They appear to have the right beliefs. They may be working hard in the church. They're deacons. Elders. Ushers. Church van drivers. Church secretaries. Small group leaders. Sunday school teachers. Sometimes even pastors. They see themselves as slaves to God and do their work out of duty, but they don't grasp a true love relationship with the Father. They don't love their brothers and sisters. They're living with the Father, but their hearts are far from Him.

And the results of the prodigal's lifestyle and heart attitudes are heartbreaking.

I have so many stories of ministering to prodigals, it's hard to choose a few examples. Here are several:

- A mom in our home group has a child who was a worship leader during high school. Then he went to a secular college, unprepared for the hard questions about the faith from his professors. The limited answers he had in hand just didn't stand up against their so-called intelligent arguments. The son now considers himself an atheist. Every week, this mother asks for prayer for him in our group.

- A young man I know was brought up in the faith. He was a strong leader in our church for years. As a young adult he went through several difficult dating relationships. Then he met a girl who absolutely captivated his heart. Problem: she belonged to the Jehovah's Witnesses cult. Her definition of Jesus and the gospel didn't line up with his—or the Bible's. He fell in love with her anyway, and now he goes to a Jehovah's Witnesses group and considers himself one of them.

- A middle-aged couple in our church has five daughters. For a long time, the husband and father was considered an example of Christian maturity. But he went through a midlife crisis and abandoned his wife and family. He had an affair with a woman half his age. Now she's pregnant. The whole thing is such a mess. It's caused heartbreak for many people.

- A helper at our benevolence program that feeds the hungry has been faithfully undertaking her ministry for years. But she sat down with her small group leader recently to talk about a problem with another woman in the church. They just don't get along, and there's no movement toward restoration. When the leader questioned the first woman about her relationship with the Lord, she admitted she hasn't been reading her Bible or praying. Her heart is far from the Lord. She's been serving faithfully, but that's the extent of her faith. She's been going through the motions with the Lord, but that's it.

- Christian parents have two teenagers, a boy and a girl, both raised in the church. The boy is walking with the Lord, while the girl is far from God. She is defiant, sullen, rude, and often in trouble at school. She's dating a boy who's not a believer, far from the Lord, and openly using drugs. The parents strongly suspect their daughter is sleeping with her boyfriend. The parents are so troubled. They can't understand why one of their kids is turning out so well, while the other isn't.

- One of our faithful servants in the church raised his son to know Jesus from the beginning. He was a part of our youth group and went on many mission trips. He went to college and got into a relationship with another young man. He says he is gay but is a gay Christian. The father is at a loss.

No Hopeless Prodigals

The good news is that there's help for prodigals—and for people who care about the well-being of prodigals and want to see them restored to the heart of God. As long as the prodigal is alive, there is hope because of the third son in the story—Jesus! Prodigals don't need to live their whole lives far from Christ, their biological family, and the family of God.

I'm grateful we have a lot of prodigals in and around our church so we have a chance to love them back to Christ, but I rejoice that we also have many, many prodigals who've come back to the Lord after a season or two away. We are seeing those prodigals return to walking with the Lord and being restored to their immediate family and the family of God. It's so great to witness.

Earlier I mentioned that today more than one in three millennials don't affiliate with any religion at all and some three out of four teens who currently attend church will soon drop out. Here's the encouraging twist. For some of those teens, the dropout is a hiatus, not a permanent departure.[4] But what of the rest?

Is there something we can do that might help bring the prodigal home? Can we shorten the time it takes for them to return, or remove the hiatus season altogether? There's not one magic silver bullet, one single solution. We as the spiritual parents can choose to do the right thing, but this does not guarantee the right reaction. People have free will; they walk away from the Lord for many different reasons, and return for many reasons. However, we can follow some principles on our side of the equation to make things easier for the prodigal to return, and we'll talk about these throughout this book. The overarching solution is for parents and churches to know and love the Lord and to disciple their children before children are old enough to move toward rebellion. Real discipleship that leads to spiritual maturity both defends against people walking away from Christ and helps bring people back.

Discipleship is the process where people are not only converted to the Christian faith (Matt. 28:18–19) but brought into spiritual maturity (Matt. 28:19). God uses three main vehicles for doing this: the Word of God (the Bible), the Spirit of God (the Holy Spirit), and the people of God (the physical family and the church).

The missing ingredient is often the third piece—quality spiritual relationships with other believers. Relationships with other Christians are like ropes that help bind us to the Lord and hold us fast to what's good and honorable and right and true.

Discipleship happens in relationship, and the result of being well discipled is that young believers enjoy relationship with God and other believers in both the physical and spiritual families. Without strong discipling, they don't have the strength and support that helps them unpack real questions and problems that arise from life in this spiritual war zone. They might have made a decision for Jesus at camp. Or maybe they accepted the Lord at Sunday school, but that was pretty much it. They were helped to be born again into infanthood but never spiritually parented to grow into the mature person God desired them to be. They never grew in the faith. Maybe their parents didn't disciple them because they were never discipled themselves. The parents may have thought that discipling their children was all the church's job. And the church thought that was the parents' job.

In the end, nobody was getting discipled. But there is hope.

Light One Candle

One Christmas Eve, my father, my son, and I (Jim) preached a sermon called "Passing Down Christmas." We preached the message in parts, all three of us on the platform in front of the auditorium at the same time. It was a candle-lighting service that focused on not just passing down various traditions of the Christmas season but also passing down our faith (the essence of Christmas) to our children and grandchildren.

The message started with a picture of my grandfather on the big screen and an unlit candle on the stage. My father, Bill, shared how his grandparents and parents had put a lot of effort into the Christmas celebration every year, but his father, when he died at age seventy-one, had not shared what he believed or his testimony about what Jesus had done in his life. He had not really taught his son about Jesus.

My dad had always felt far from his father, and though they all went to church, he'd grown up with no real faith. But when my dad was older and going through difficult times, nearly suicidal, an older spiritual mentor came into my dad's life who began to unpack the traditions his parents had introduced through church and Christmas, but never really explained. My dad married, I was born, and my parents began to do things differently. Dad's goal was to light my candle of faith from the beginning. He started a new kind of Christmas and a new kind of legacy in our family.

I then talked about what my dad and mom had done with me. They had tried to plant some really good seeds of faith in my life. But in my free will, I chose to reject the faith as I got older. I walked away from the Lord and became an alcoholic and an atheist who hurt my parents (and myself) in many ways. But my father never gave up on me and pursued me. Though he was a preacher, I was not won back through Dad's preaching. I was won back through his and my mother's selfless love and grace. With their help, I tried to do things wisely in the life of my son.

Bill's Notes for Deeper Reflection

Which of the THREE SONS are you most like?

As you think over the biblical account of the prodigal son from Luke 15:11–32, ask yourself, which son are you most like in the story—the younger son, the older son, or Jesus? You may want to go through this quiz twice: once for yourself and once for the prodigal in your life as you pray for this person. Why? Because it helps breed compassion and empathy to admit that we have all gone astray. It also acts as a warning, for any one of us is susceptible to falling away from the truth. Check all that apply.

The Younger Son (The Outward Prodigal)

1. He Lost the Battle for His Thoughts

____ He looked out from home

____ He became discontent

____ He became self-centered

____ He became filled with lust and greed

2. He Lost the Battle of His Behavior

____ He acted on sinful thoughts

____ He disrespected his father

____ He left his family

____ He put his family's values behind him

3. He Lost the Battle of His Habits

____ He willfully headed toward evil

____ He willfully repeated harmful actions

____ He developed harmful habits

4. He Faced the Consequences of His Choices

____ He lost relationships with family

____ He lost his home

____ He lost his money

____ He made—then lost—false friends

____ He grew jealous of pigs

5. He Was Convicted of His Own Sin

___ He realized he had sinned against heaven

___ He realized he had sinned against his father

___ He experienced a deep sense of loss

___ He grew jealous of his father's servants

6. He Was Repentant

___ He had a change of mind

___ He was sorry enough for his sin to want to change

7. He Chose to Act on His Repentance

___ He said, "I will arise and go to my father"

___ He headed in the direction of home

8. He Chose to Return

___ He allowed himself to be embraced by the father

___ He allowed himself to be celebrated by the father

The Older Son (The Inward Prodigal)

9. He Lost the Battle for His Thoughts

___ He began to be proud of being better than his brother

___ He became critical and judgmental

10. He Lost the Battle for His Behavior

___ His lack of love for his brother exhibited itself in disgust

___ Because of his lack of love, he withdrew from people

___ He made a list of his brother's sins and held on to his list

___ Because of his lack of love, he was angry, simmering until he exploded

11. He Lost the Battle for His Habits

___ He focused on all his brother had done, or not done, that hurt his family

___ He refused to forgive

12. He Faced the Consequences of His Actions

___ He missed out on the party

___ He accused his father of favoritism

____ He separated himself from his family and friends

____ He became bitter

____ His felt like a slave instead of a son

13. He Was Convicted of His Own Sin

His father held up his sin to him, showing him . . .

____ He did not love his family members

____ He was angry when he should have been rejoicing

____ He was carrying a grudge when he could have enjoyed all the father offered

14. He Should Have Repented of His Own Sin

____ His focus was on his brother's sin, not his own

15. He Should Have Focused on Healing and Restoration (Matt. 7:1–5; 18:1–35)

____ He remained focused on his brother's sin, not his own need

16. He Should Have Been Restored to His Family (Matt. 18:11, 17)

____ He stayed unforgiving

____ He lost the joy of celebration

The Good Father (God/Jesus) (1 Cor. 13:4–8)

____ He was patient, kind, not jealous or boastful

____ He wasn't proud, rude, or irritable

____ He did not demand his own way

____ He did not keep a record of wrongs

____ He didn't rejoice in injustice but rejoiced when truth won out

____ He never gave up, never lost hope, and never quit loving

____ He watched for his son's return

____ He was full of grace and love and forgiveness

____ He forgave and restored his son

____ He sought to restore his other prodigal son

____ He celebrated restoration in his family

At this point my son shared how he had believed when he was young but later rejected the faith and became a drug addict. He overdosed and almost died, he ran away from home, spent time in jail and rehab programs, and landed in a homeless shelter. But with the help of family and church, God strengthened my wife and me. And together, we were able to win him back.

My son then shared what Lori and I and my father and mother had done in his life, and how it softened his heart and how he returned. He shared that there were consequences of his rebellion for sure—he did not graduate from high school and had a son out of wedlock with a woman he hardly knew. He shared how God had worked it all out so that now he was a youth minister working with kids who had drug problems. Now he was married and had a son with his believing wife.

As each of us in turn talked about what had happened and how God had helped to save our kids, we lit a candle. In the end, my son's four-year-old son, Kaden (the son born out of wedlock), came up and had his candle lit. Kaden then went to the crowd and lit one person's candle. That person lit another person's candle, and so on and so on, until every person in the auditorium had a lit candle. The house lights were off, and it was an amazing sight to see row after row of candles glowing in the dark. So many in our church had known of our struggle to save our son. They had prayed for us and sought to help in so many ways as a church family—we had all prayerfully helped to bring my son home. Now as a church we wanted to help provide a new future for Kaden, just the same way as we prayerfully commit to helping everyone walk closely with the Lord.

Throughout this book, we're going to prayerfully help you with the prodigal in your life, the prodigal whom you focus most upon. I wish I could say there's one magic formula, but life is not like that. Life can be messy and complicated. I get that. And I know that statistics are not merely numbers. Statistics represent real people. The people who have walked away from God are our children, our friends, our family members, our neighbors, our classmates, people we once worked with at camp, maybe even our mentors or parents or spouses, people we care about the most. Our prayer is that these prodigals would come to their senses and return home to the Father. Why should we care? Why should we make it our mission to do all in our power to woo prodigals back to the Father? Because these people are loved by our Father and we love Him. In some respects we were all prodigals and He came for us. And when we love the Father, we remember that we were first loved by Him, and those people out there are loved as well. They are God's creation, and He wants them to become a part of His spiritual family through faith in Christ. They are dead and lost, and God wants them alive and found.

The good news is that the Father is already looking for them, actively waiting for their return. He's fully prepared to sprint down the road toward them, greet them in a loving embrace, and say, "Welcome home!"

PART I

THE
IDEAL

2

Building a Home
That's Hard to Leave

When I (Jim) was young, my dad pastored a church that rented a building used for other purposes during the week. Each Sunday morning we helped Dad set up "church" by hooking up sound equipment, setting up chairs, and getting the pulpit in place. Each Sunday afternoon, we helped tear it all down. We worked with a bunch of volunteers that Dad had enlisted.

Sunday mornings can be a stressful time for any preacher. He's got a lot on his mind. He's praying about who will attend (or who won't). He's running through his sermon in his mind again. He might be worried about the budget or a hard conversation with someone or complaints about the music or the length of his message. There's a lot that can stress out a pastor.

One morning as we helped Dad set up church, a volunteer did something dumb—I don't remember what it was—and Dad yelled at him. I mean, Dad gave him a real verbal lashing. The guy realized he'd done something stupid and mumbled he wouldn't do it again. But the rebuke Dad gave him was larger than the offense.

By the time Dad started preaching that morning, the Holy Spirit must have been really convicting him, because about five minutes into his sermon, Dad completely stopped. For a few seconds that seemed like forever, there was absolute silence. You could have heard a pin drop. Then Dad said, "I've got nothing to say until I ask a member of this congregation for forgiveness." Right there, in front of everybody, Dad said, "Every week you come and serve, and what did you get for it? Me criticizing you. God is proud of you and so am I." He asked for forgiveness, thanked the man for being a faithful volunteer, then went back to preaching where he had left off.

Over my lifetime, I've heard my dad preach hundreds of sermons. Maybe thousands. But the sermon he preached that day reached the top five that spoke the loudest. He preached through the genuineness of his repentance and humility. I saw my father as a man who wasn't perfect—and that was okay. I saw sincerity. Dad wasn't a hypocrite. It was one of the best things Dad did in building a home that was hard for me to leave. And later on, it made it easier to come home to.

No home is a perfect home. Not in the real world. And even if a home is excellent, that doesn't guarantee that a child won't become a prodigal. But with Christ's help, we can build homes that are hard to leave.

Maybe your child has already gone astray. If so, then the rest of this book is for you, but this first section is for the person who understands that preventative tools are even better than reactionary ones. You are still at a place where prevention is possible. So before we start down the road of winning the prodigal back, let's look at what makes it hard for them to leave and easier to come back. Maybe your children are on the edge, and a few adjustments will make your home more stable and secure.

Two big questions:

How do you build a home that's hard to leave?

How do you rebuild a home for your prodigal to return to?

Why do prodigals leave in the first place? There is no one answer other than their relationship with God isn't firmly established. My dad says, "There was only one thing wrong with my son, but because that one thing was wrong, nothing much was right. He didn't have a right relationship with the Father through Jesus the Son."

A multitude of secondary reasons exist, and the fuller reason is often a combination. In fact, the reasons may be symptomatic of a deeper problem. For instance, alcohol is usually not a root cause; it's a symptom. The root cause is some deeper pain or disappointment or outright choice to rebel. The problem exhibits itself through alcohol use.

A person might become a prodigal for intellectual reasons. The prodigal wasn't given the right tools to correctly grasp the faith and is led astray by pseudo-intellectual arguments that convince the child that God isn't real or that Jesus isn't the only way to God.

A person might become a prodigal because of moral issues. The lure of the world feels too powerful, and whether gradually or quickly, the person is sucked into immoral living. Some strong temptation presents itself—maybe drugs or sexual sins or lust for possessions—and the person chooses to succumb to that temptation and walk away from the Lord.

A person might encounter hypocrisy in other Christians and not have the maturity yet to distinguish it from real faith, so he assumes that all Christians are hypocrites and walks away.

A person might become a prodigal because she has been hurt. This prodigal is not rebelling so much as desperately seeking love or healing or approval or security or acceptance. The person goes to the wrong source for comfort and in the process walks away from God.

Free will always plays a role. Thanks to free will, nothing is guaranteed. You may do everything possible to build a strong home, yet a person may still become a prodigal by free choice. The lifestyle of friends or the culture looks inviting, so they choose to go that direction. A teenage boy wants to be cool, so he hangs out with the wrong friends and they lead him astray. A teenage girl wants to be loved and wants her self-esteem pumped up by having a boyfriend. Along comes a guy who is bad news, but she dates him because she feels flattered and is swept off her feet. Or an adult chooses to have an affair because he justifies that his needs aren't being met at home or because there's chaos at home. Free will is a factor in all of these decisions.

Again, the root problem in every prodigal's experience is that their relationship with the Lord isn't what it needs to be. They may know about the Lord but not have surrendered to Him as their Savior and Lord. They may have received Christ but have not been discipled into maturity. Their relational ropes are not securely fastened. A big part of safeguarding against the prodigal problem is building a home that's hard to leave—or a home that can be returned to after going astray.

The Prodigal and God's Law

So, what does the ideal home look like? It starts with accepting the Lord as the architect of your spiritual house. Jesus said a foolish man hears God's Word but builds his house on sand rather than rock, and when the storm comes, the house crashes.

We must understand Psalm 127:1: "Unless the LORD builds the house, the builders labor in vain." This construction work happens when we

- submit to Christ as Lord
- surrender to the Holy Spirit
- commit our way to the Lord and align our lives with Scripture, seeking His wisdom in prayer
- commit ourselves to be a part of God's family, the church
- seek godly counsel from older, wiser people in the church
- help our kids develop godly friendships

Then the Lord is building our house.

A great part of the ideal home is helping our children understand that their value and identity aren't in what they do but in who they are in Christ. Jesus, the grace giver, loves unconditionally.

To understand this, we need to see the story of the prodigal son as a picture of how God works. As Jesus narrates the story, the Son of God constantly points us to His Father, describing righteous character. Jesus shows us the graciousness, love, compassion, justice, and mercy of God. When the religious leaders heard Jesus's teaching, it sounded so foreign, they had to be shocked. As Jesus told about the son declaring he wanted his father's things before his death, you can imagine their indignation. They thought the father would give him an earful. Instead, the actual response of the father had to leave them befuddled. In that ancient culture, Mosaic law allowed parents to kill a rebellious son. Deuteronomy 21:18–21 contains this strong directive:

> If someone has a stubborn and rebellious son who does not obey his father and mother and will not listen to them when they discipline him, his father and mother shall take hold of him and bring him to the elders at the gate of his town. They shall say to the elders, "This son of ours is stubborn and rebellious. He will not obey us. He is a glutton and a drunkard." Then all the men of his town are to stone him to death. You must purge the evil from among you. All Israel will hear of it and be afraid.

If your son had gone astray and would not repent in those days, then you stoned him. You definitely didn't let him take your possessions and leave. You surely didn't let him come home again. There was no new ring for his finger. No new cloak or shoes. No party and celebration of his return.

What a surprise to the ancient Jewish listeners that the good father acted as he did with the prodigal son. Even the Lord's disciples were confused. They were only beginning to see that Jesus came not to abolish the law, but to fulfill it (Matt. 5:17–20). Fulfillment of the law was the heart of Jesus's message. Jesus wasn't setting Himself up to contradict the law but to fulfill it and provide relief from it.

See, the law was given to the Israelites to make them aware of sin. God knew that nobody could perfectly obey the law, that this standard of perfection was impossible for us to meet because of our sinful nature. The law also revealed God's willingness to accept a substitute for the law's penalty, the sacrificial lamb to cover our sins. So both God's righteousness and His heart of love are revealed in the law. In Christ we see the Lamb of God willingly sacrifice Himself to save those He loves (2 Cor. 5:21). Paul clarifies: "No one will be declared righteous in God's sight by the works of the law; rather, through the law we become conscious of our sin" (Rom. 3:20). "Christ is the culmination of the law so that there may be righteousness for everyone who believes" (Rom. 10:4).

In other words, the real reason for the law is that people would look at it and understand their need for a Savior. John Piper puts it this way: "The ultimate goal of the law is that we would look to Christ, not law-keeping, for our righteousness. . . . Let us worship the wonder of Christ who unleashed these massive changes in the world."[1]

As children absorb this truth little by little, under the parents' unconditional love, they see themselves valued for who they are, not for how they perform or meet the house rules.

We Are All Prodigals

If you think about it, you can see that the prodigal son story is really just a different way to tell the story of creation and planet Earth. We live in a prodigal world. We have a prodigal planet of our own making. God allows rebellion to exist in hopes that prodigal people come to their senses and find their way home to Him.

This can be a difficult concept to grasp. Often the biggest barrier atheists set up between themselves and God is that they can't understand why a good God would allow evil to exist. The straightforward answer is that God, in His love, allows us to experience the consequences of our own decisions.

Think of it this way: In the beginning, before the fall, God, the perfect Father, walked in perfect relationship with humankind. Yet God gave us free will. God didn't want robots who had no say in the matter. He wanted us to love and follow Him of our own free will. He is a relational God who has been in relationship within the Trinity for eternity. To be made in His image is to be made relational by nature. So God gave us the ability that He has—the ability to choose love and relationship. He set one tree in the midst of the Garden of Eden and said, "You can eat from any other tree, just not this one" (Gen. 2:16–17). It was a test, because free will must be allowed choices or it's not free.

Satan, in serpent form, tempted Eve first. She failed the test, ate the fruit, and disobeyed God. Adam ate the fruit too and also failed the test. In that failure, it was as if humankind—us (because each of us in our own time failed our test)—was saying to God, "We don't trust You; we don't want Your rules; we want to do our own thing, we trust our own perspective more than Yours." How do we know we are in this narrative too? The Bible says we are all "in" Adam. In a sense, we're all chips off the same block. Romans 5:12 says, "Sin entered the world through one man, and death through sin, and in this way death came to all people, because all sinned." So we are all prodigals. We have all sinned and fallen short of the glory of God (Rom. 3:23). How's this for a thought? Even the most perfect Father has prodigal children. He didn't do anything wrong as a "parent," and yet His children use their gift of free will to go against Him.

How do all of us prodigals get so lost? Notice the progression in Romans 1:18–32: God creates us and places within us the knowledge that He is God. But people suppress that knowledge, refuse to worship Him or even give Him thanks. Then they think up foolish ideas to explain away God. Their minds become dark and confused, and they turn to worshiping idols and creatures God made. God steps aside and quits convicting, allowing them to act out their sinful thoughts. The next downward step trades the truth about God for lies, and He again steps aside and lets them experience the consequences of sinful choices, which spiral ever downward. Despite knowledge of God's judgment, they continue in sin and encourage others to sin with them. Because of the knowledge God gave at the beginning, they have no excuse (Rom. 1:20).

Why does God allow the world to continue in such a sorry state? It's because God wants us to experience our own kingship—and know that it doesn't work. Without Christ, we try to be our own lords. We try to do our own thing. But this only causes chaos and confusion, sorrow and heartbreak. The Father knows that not being in fellowship with Him won't work. But life under our own lordship helps us recognize that life with the Father is good. God allows us to leave His spiritual house (depicted by the Garden of Eden) so we can discover with our free will the truth of the world without Him. All in hopes that we will come home of our own free will.

It's actually a loving God who allows this. And it's humbling to realize we've all walked the prodigal road in some measure.

Four Factors of a Winsome Home

Now let's see how these biblical principles apply to building an ideal home. From the account of the prodigal son in Luke 15:11–31, we can see that a home that is hard to leave but easy to return to is a home where four practical factors are followed:

> *1. People in the family are valued more highly*
> *than possessions.*

Notice the son came freely to talk to his father about his plans, telling us that communication was an established wall of the home's foundation. A hard discussion, yes, but they knew how to talk to each other. That makes a home hard to leave.

Which was more important to the prodigal's father—possessions or his son? When the son asked for his full share of the inheritance, if possessions were valued more than people, the father would have just said no. But this was not the case in this home. That father's eyes were on his son.

What if the father's reputation in his community had been more important than his son? In that culture, things like this got around. There'd be talk in the town—people would question the father's parenting style. They'd second-guess the father's response, suggesting he should have done this or that. But the father wasn't concerned about wealth or reputation—he'd lose it all if he could gain his son. The father valued his son even to the point of letting him learn a lesson the hard way. The father was willing to let go of possessions and reputation for the sake of a son he hoped would someday come home.

We have discovered what was most important to the prodigal's father. What is most important to you? When it comes to you and your prodigal, what might it look like for you to give love like the prodigal's father, like our heavenly Father?

When we apply this principle and value people more than possessions, and relationship over reputation, it may mean we work less in order to spend more time with people in our home. Sure, work is important and needs to get done. But maybe we shouldn't work so much overtime, or perhaps our spouse shouldn't have a job outside of the home for a season, or perhaps we can say no to extra work, hobbies, and even roles in the church. Some couples deliberately choose for the wife not to work full-time outside the home while they raise their children. That may mean a stretch of time from a child's birth through high school graduation so one parent is consistently there for the children. Perhaps it simply means we learn to unplug from work at the end of each day so we can focus on our family with greater attentiveness.

2. People in the family are treated fairly.

The good father practiced treating everyone fairly in and outside his home. Even his servants were valued. We know this because when the prodigal son had hit rock bottom and contemplated eating with the pigs, he remembered how well his father's servants had it back home.

What if we modeled loving and treating everyone with respect in our homes, churches, workplaces, and culture? What might it look like? The father was consistent—he didn't preach one thing at home but then treat his employees with disdain.

We don't have servants today, but we have people who perform all sorts of humble tasks for us. People who bring us meals in restaurants. People who bag our groceries. Are we treating everyone well—from the clerk to the bus driver to the kid who knocks on our door selling cookies?

Our children's friends are valuable. Learn their names. Get to know them. Our children's teachers are valuable. Make a point to attend school events. When we model the Father's love and respect for everyone, our children will know that even if they become prodigals, they can always come home to find a place of grace, forgiveness, restoration, peace, fun, safety, and security, rather than a place of harsh words and tension.

3. Prodigals are loved no matter what they have done.

Love reigns throughout the good father's home. We see this when the son initially leaves. The father obviously knows something is wrong in his son's heart as he makes his unreasonable request. He listens and responds in a way that seems grace filled and thoughtful. Though the father is obviously hurt, no threats are mentioned to scare or coerce the child or tell the child that if he does this, he is ruined forever.

The father represents God, who always knows the harsh consequences a wayward son will face. Many of us know by personal experience that a prodigal faces consequences. He will eventually become miserable. But even then, the father in the story never stops loving the boy. The father is always watching, constantly waiting for his return.

When the son comes home, a great celebration is held, but the father and the returned prodigal both know there are still consequences for his actions. Relationships will need to be repaired. The boy's inheritance is squandered, and the father had already given the rest of the inheritance to the older son. We see no evidence of the father dishing out more money, but he gives the son full love and restoration. Humans will often allow bitterness to rub past hurt and current consequences in the faces of those who have returned. Not so with the heavenly Father. There will be consequences, but the Father loves us through them without reminding us of our sin.

What happens in our homes when we love our children no matter what they do? Does it go beyond forgiving past behavior? Does it offer a restoration process, and if so, what does that look like? Does it mean we allow them to continue to rebel in our homes? How do their consequences impact the family? Hard, individual questions.

Certainly actions have consequences, and our love doesn't erase them. Rebellion hurts everyone in some way, because that's the way rebellion works. But the Father loves unconditionally and we reinforce that with our own unconditional love. If we love like Jesus, we let our children choose, but we love them more than our possessions and no matter what they do. This kind of love makes it possible for them to come home and be restored.

Surely this is how Christ works with us. "All we like sheep have gone astray" (Isa. 53:6 ESV), yet "while we were still sinners, Christ died for us" (Rom. 5:8). Jesus doesn't love us because we're presentable to Him. He doesn't love us because we are shined up, perfect, ready and able and willing to do good works. No, He loves us in spite of our sins. He works to restore us to the Father, always loving us, always caring for us, always welcoming us home.

God not only loves us with a love that can be measured, but He wants us to love others with the same love He gives us. Ask yourself these hard questions:

Do you love your family **because** they are good?
Do you love your family **if** they do good?
Do you love your family **in spite of** what they do?
Or do you love your family **no matter what**?

4. Grace and forgiveness are extended to all the prodigals in the home.

Often when the prodigal comes home, other family members express lack of love or forgiveness. In our story, it's the older son with this problem. But the father steps in to offer the same love and grace to him also. Scripture doesn't tell us if he accepts it. Initially, the older brother displays bitterness and hurt, envy and anger. The younger brother had caused chaos in the family while the older brother played the part of the good son, but in his heart he is just as far from the father as his younger brother. He had stayed home and worked, but he wasn't grateful for all he had been given. He tells his father he had slaved for him and received nothing. Yet he too would be receiving a large inheritance. He may have stayed at home with the father, but he certainly didn't have the heart of the father.

The behavior of a prodigal affects everyone in the family, and if there are two prodigals, we have twice the opportunity to have the conversations that help restore them. We must never sweep sin under the rug, but extending grace means that if sin is genuinely confessed, we genuinely forgive.

Note that the younger brother genuinely confesses his sin. He comes to his senses and declares that he will return to his father and say, "Father, I have sinned against heaven and against you" (Luke 15:21). The younger son realizes the consequences of his actions. He does not believe he is even worthy to be called a son. He can only hope his father would make him a hired servant.

But the father has other plans. He hugs his son and welcomes him home. He gives him a ring for his finger and sandals for his feet. He throws a party in his honor.

What would it look like for our grace and forgiveness to contain this kind of joy, celebration, and restoration? A pattern starts in smaller matters. If a child sins against us, then how do we respond? Are our standards clear? Is there a sense of celebration following repentance and forgiveness when a child is age four or ten or fourteen? This sets a pattern in a young child's mind so they'll be familiar with the road to restoration. They'll know their home is one where grace is extended. That very knowing may prevent their heading down the prodigal road.

Discipleship in the Home

What does this ideal home—hard to leave and easy to come home to—look like? This home has love and relationship, boundaries for our own good, and respect for all. People are loved no matter what, and there are restoring conversations, grace, and forgiveness in action. In a nutshell, real discipleship is occurring. People are being helped to draw closer and closer to Jesus. People are constantly growing in spiritual maturity, which encompasses real love between siblings.

A home that is hard to leave but easy to come home to is a place where we provide for our children the real version of Christianity—not a false version that's harsh and unforgiving and tough to be around. That's what the religious leaders and older brother were like. Instead, we need to show our children the Christianity that's authentic, full of grace and truth. For example, do our children see us keep our own accounts short? Do they hear us apologize when we've slipped up and ask for forgiveness when we need to?

If we want to rescue our children, then we need to start with ourselves. As individuals. As parents. As children of God. When our relationship with God is healthy, then we can disciple (model, teach, instruct, and discipline) our children to know the Lord and build an authentic faith. Modeling for them a false or unhealthy version of the faith only provokes our children to anger, and we are told not to exasperate our children. Instead, we are to bring them up in the training and instruction of the Lord (Eph. 6:4). The Amplified Bible states Ephesians 6:4 this way:

> Fathers, do not provoke your children to anger [do not exasperate them to the point of resentment with demands that are trivial or unreasonable or humiliating or abusive; nor by showing favoritism or indifference to any of them], but bring them up [tenderly, with lovingkindness] in the discipline and instruction of the Lord.

Look at the various components of that verse. Try to picture what each of these principles will look like in your home:

- Don't exasperate them with trivial or unreasonable demands
- Don't humiliate them
- Don't be physically or emotionally abusive
- Don't show favoritism

- Don't show indifference
- Bring them up tenderly
- Bring them up with loving-kindness
- Bring them up in the discipline and instruction of the Lord

Think about it this way. Many parents hear that they need to create a home that honors God. So they falsely assume that means a home that's a no-fun zone. It's a home of harsh rules and regulations. A home of rigidity and inflexibility. In this home you must look a certain way, act a certain way, or think a certain way, and you definitely must behave a certain way and avoid embarrassing the family by making a public mistake.

But discipleship starts with looking at how Jesus called His first disciples. This is the template for what Jesus wants for all of His followers—then and now.

> While walking by the Sea of Galilee, he [Jesus] saw two brothers, Simon (who is called Peter) and Andrew his brother, casting a net into the sea, for they were fishermen. And he said to them, "Follow me, and I will make you fishers of men." (Matt. 4:18–20 ESV)

Those three verses form the essence of true discipleship—and also the essence of what a home that follows Jesus is all about. We are to build a relational faith in our homes, not merely an intellectual faith. We are to center our lives on the person and work of Jesus Christ. We are invited to have an intimate relationship with Jesus and do life together with Him and other believers. Our faith is not just about facts. It's not just about serving. It's not merely about Bible knowledge. It's a faith of relationship and discipleship.

Look at three important directives in Matthew 4:18–20:

1. **We are to follow Jesus.** Jesus wants us to make this our number one personal priority: following Him. The next verse says that "immediately they left their nets and followed him" (v. 21). Are we following anything other than Jesus? Do we go to anything other than Jesus to find salvation, peace, comfort, security, or identity? Jesus wants to be Lord of our lives. Likewise, we are to train our children to follow Jesus wholeheartedly by showing them what that looks like.

2. **We are to let Jesus transform us.** Jesus said, "I will make you fishers of men." This means that Christ will take us as we are but will begin to do a work in our lives. Because Jesus loves us so much, He isn't content to leave us in our sin. He's molding our lives, shaping our characters. Second Corinthians 3:18 says, "And we all, who with unveiled faces contemplate the Lord's glory, are being transformed into his image with ever-increasing glory." Are we constantly encouraging our children to be transformed by Jesus? He is the perfect picture of spiritual maturity. All the law and the prophets are summed up in two commands—love God and love others. Jesus is showing us how to become relationship experts who love well.

3. **We are to join Jesus in His mission.** Jesus transforms His disciples into "fishers of men." That means He has a job for us to do, a calling for us to live out. He wants to transform His disciples into disciples who make other disciples and love those who are lost prodigals. We aren't merely to accept Christ, then rest on our laurels. Are we

constantly encouraging our children to find their place of service in the body of Christ, becoming disciples who make disciples?

That's how we build a home that's hard to leave but easy to come home to. We disciple our children to know they're loved by Christ. They find purpose in Christ. They're rooted and established in Him (Col. 3:17–19). They're joined with other believers in many God-honoring relationships. This all makes it hard to leave, but if they do leave, when they come to themselves, they will know they can come home.

God's Ideal

As Jim and I (Bill) close this chapter, I want to say that we're not writing because we're experts at having the ideal home. Both he and I have made a lot of mistakes along the way, and we're writing to you not out of our successes but out of our failures, out of what we learned, out of the grace and mercy that God allowed in our lives.

I always wanted to be a good dad. I wanted my son and me to be friends. But my own father had made his share of mistakes, so when it came to being a dad, I really had little clue of even where to begin. My wife, Bobbi, and I got married when we were young and had five children in six years. Jim was the oldest, then four daughters: Melissa, Joni, Angela, and Melody. It was a real zoo in our house for a long time. Bobbi and I were both Christians, and I served in pastoral ministry for most of those years and was head of a statewide ministry organization, but neither of us as parents really knew what it meant to disciple our children, to lead them to love Jesus, to let Jesus transform

Bill's Notes for Deeper Reflection
Job Description for Christian Parents

What can you do when there is nothing more you can do? When you can't go back and fix what you've broken? When you are overwhelmed with the present? When you are living in fear of the future? Check whether you are operating on a faulty job description or the biblical job description for parents.

The Faulty Job Description for Christian Parents

The wrong job description is an if/then equation. It's a whole false belief system that says **if** you are a good enough parent, **then** you will be able to save your children. **If** you try harder, **then** your children will come home. **If** you pray more, read more, discipline more, **then** your children will turn out to be good Christians.

Watch out for the trap. The if/then job description will only break your heart. This is truth: **if** your children could become Christians by your good parenting alone, **then** they wouldn't need a Savior.

The Bible's Job Description for Christian Parents

Our children are never fully ours. They are on loan to us from the Lord. Our children belong to Him. They are His children first, and God loves our children more than we will ever love them—and we love them a lot!

Our job is to partner with God in His mission to raise children who become wholehearted followers of Christ. Our responsibility is greatest when they are younger. It's to teach and model for them what it is to believe in Jesus. To show them that they belong to a body of believers. To explain to them and encourage them that Jesus transforms lives. And to help guide them toward joining Jesus on His mission.

As they get older, their personal responsibility in this becomes greater and ours as parents becomes less. We need to release them while still maintaining the relationship. We need to be available for them to talk, to encourage them, and to pray for them.

their lives, and to encourage our children to join with Jesus on His mission.

At the beginning of our parenting, we had high expectations that all of our children would love the Lord, love us, and love each other, but as we fell apart, I just hoped that we would survive. For one period of time, when Jim was a teen, it felt like nearly everyone in our family was in crisis. Jim was in rebellion. So was one of our daughters. Another daughter was unmarried and pregnant. And due to unforeseen doctor's bills, Bobbi and I were $96,000 in debt. Our dreams had turned into nightmares, and there was no way we could ever dig ourselves out of this hole.

I basically had a complete emotional collapse and lay on my bed for two weeks, then went to a counselor. I tell you that because I know what it feels like to be in crisis—and if that's how you're feeling right now, then I want you to know you're not alone. I look back at some of the big mistakes I made along the way as a parent. I'm an insecure guy, and I tried to make up for my insecurity as a parent by trying too hard. In all my trying I just about drove my family away and drove myself nuts.

One day in the middle of all our crises, in the waiting room of my doctor's office, I picked up a random copy of *Reader's Digest*. I found an article with a prayer that said, "Lord, when I wake up in the middle of the night and don't know where my child is, or what they are doing, please help me remember that You love my child even more than I do." I confess I tore that page right out of the *Reader's Digest*, folded it up, and carried it in my wallet for years. That became a touchstone for me, a promise to remember for always. God loved my children even more than I did. Bobbi and I didn't need to do this parenting thing alone. We were invited to do it in partnership with God.

How did we survive? Bobbi and I made the decision that we needed to rebuild our home on the rock of Jesus Christ. We needed to rebuild a home that the younger ones wouldn't want to leave and where the older ones would want to come back. For a while, life was still pretty hard. Bobbi got up at five in the morning and prayed. I wrote pages and pages in my journal, prayers to God mostly. Bobbi and I asked ourselves all the hard questions about our kids, trying to head off problems before they came up. Bobbi and I started having weekly dates and a time away each month, just us, to remember why we got married. And we consistently worked to love and pray for our prodigal kids. Although we set boundaries for them, the door was never shut. If they would accept those boundaries, they were always welcome to come home. And the church helped out in big ways. Instead of firing me, they pitched in and prayed for us. Our church family never left us.

If you're in crisis right now due to a prodigal in your life, please know there's hope. Jesus Christ, the Great Physician, can work through you to rebuild a home for your prodigals to come home to. He can heal wounds. God can help you pay back seemingly insurmountable debt, like He did for us. Broken families can be put back together. Rebellious children can soften and turn from their sinful ways. They can be restored and follow Christ wholeheartedly.

I say all that because I've lived all that. We have a great Father in heaven who loves our children and family even more than we do as parents. There's real hope in Him.

3

Building a Church
That's Hard to Leave

When my (Jim's) son and daughter-in-law were recently married, I glanced around at the wedding party and at the guests, and it struck me just how connected my son and daughter-in-law were to the church. My son's groomsmen had grown up with him in youth group. My daughter-in-law's attendants had grown up with her in youth group. Most importantly, the two had met on a youth group missions trip that turned out to be the trip of their lives. A bunch of friends were there from our church who had connected with them through all kinds of touch points in their lives. I saw past teachers from the Christian school in our church, small group leaders, hunting partners, parents of their friends. Lori and I saw people from our current and past small groups, people we'd prayed with and people we'd gone on vacation with. The smiling faces, the laughter, the memories—it was like a family reunion that you actually wanted to be at.

Over the years, those relationships had acted like ropes that bound this wedding couple to other brothers and sisters in the Lord—relational, emotional, and spiritual ropes that helped them grow in the faith and come back to the Lord when they strayed. These voices had reinforced what Lori and I had taught when our kids didn't want to hear it. These people had made my son feel forgiven when he confessed and helped these young people eventually become mature disciples of Jesus. It truly had been a village that had brought these two kids together in such an amazingly godly way. We had experienced the spiritual family the way it was supposed to be. As I pondered this, I was so glad we had taken the time to be a part of a spiritual family and so thankful for our church family.

There are three big ideas that we want to surface in this chapter. The first big idea is DON'T GO IT ALONE! Let me repeat: don't go it alone. If you have a prodigal in your life, then there's always a temptation to isolate yourself from others and crawl away in a cave somewhere. But the church was designed to help you. Let your church family help you in this experience. Reach out to them. Let them minister to you and pray for you during this time. Receive their love for you, and if the church you attend is not a safe place where grace and love is given, get involved and help it become one.

The second big idea is the importance of preventative measures. Part of the job of raising children is to model to them how to BUILD GODLY RELATIONSHIPS binding us to the Lord and His family. Building godly relationships creates many positive ties in our children's spiritual community; it makes it very hard for them to sever the ties and isolate themselves.

The third idea is our responsibility to other brothers and sisters in the body to BE THERE WHEN THEY ARE IN CRISIS. We do this by building relationships long before there is a problem. We hug the kids as they come into church when they are small. We notice and talk to them when they come to Life Group. We play around and show attention and affection as we spend time with their families. Maybe we volunteer in the children's ministry or youth group. When our kids bring home their friends, we take time to get to know them. We take them hunting or to a game with our kids. We build relational ropes with the kids to help their parents when struggles come—and they often will. As spiritually mature parents and family members, part of our job as Jesus's disciples is to provide a web of relationships for each other in crisis. God calls and commands His people to be connected, and we need to connect across age groups and levels of maturity.

Let's unpack these ideas together. How do we use them to create a church that's hard to leave?

Biblical Foundation of Effective Churches

The concept of being a "family of God" is found all through the Bible. For instance, Ephesians 2:18–20 states,

> For through him we both have access to the Father by one Spirit. Consequently, you are no longer foreigners and strangers, but fellow citizens with God's people and also members

of his household, built on the foundation of the apostles and prophets, with Christ Jesus himself as the chief cornerstone.

That passage means that all believers are unified through Jesus Christ, which should lead to practical connectedness. We all have access to God the Father by the power of the same Holy Spirit working inside of us. As such, we are not strangers or merely people who recognize each other in the church crowd. Because God is our Father, we are family. First Corinthians 12:12–27 underscores this idea, likening the followers of Christ to a spiritual body, with Christ as the head. All parts of the body need one another, and "if one part suffers, every part suffers with it; if one part is honored, every part rejoices with it" (v. 26).

Are we aware that God expects us to love our brothers and sisters as He does? Often, people hear the gospel, respond to the message that Jesus saves, and are born again, but forget they were born into a family. They think that faith is solitary and they don't need others. This mentality exists primarily in the United States, where we are taught to be fiercely independent, and in independent churches, where we are taught to give lesser importance to the church. So we may attend church, hear messages from the Scriptures, diligently read our Bibles, and pray alone, hoping to become mature in the faith by ourselves. We may even brag to others about our close and solitary relationship with God. "It's 'Jesus and me,'" we'll say, as if this was something to be proud of.

But the "Jesus and me" I-don't-need-other-Christians mentality is sorely lacking ingredients we need to become mature in our faith. Now, it's true that we need a firm foundation of scriptural knowledge and an individual experience of Bible reading and prayer. Yet to become mature, believers need a spiritual family too. The entire Bible points us to relationship—not just with God, but relationship with other believers. In Matthew 22:36–40, Jesus was asked which is the greatest commandment. "Jesus replied: 'Love the Lord your God with all your heart and with all your soul and with all your mind.' This is the first and greatest commandment. And the second is like it: 'Love your neighbor as yourself.' All the Law and the Prophets hang on these two commandments." We were created to love God and love others.

This idea continues throughout the Epistles. For instance, all the way through Ephesians we find the intertwined themes of loving God and loving others. Paul unpacks these themes when he writes, "Be completely humble and gentle; be patient, bearing with one another in love. Make every effort to keep the unity of the Spirit through the bond of peace. There is one body and one Spirit, just as you were called to one hope when you were called; one Lord, one faith, one baptism; one God and Father of all, who is over all and through all and in all" (Eph. 4:2–6).

Often, we make the mistake of equating spiritual maturity with our biblical knowledge. But maturity is not packaged in mere knowledge. Rather, it's described by our actions in loving God and loving others. If we walk with God, then we will love other people. First John 1:7 is clear: "If we walk in the light, as he is in the light, we have fellowship with one another, and the blood of Jesus, his Son, purifies us from all sin."

What Is Real Relationship?

When we talk about the necessity of "real relationship," we don't just mean shaking a few hands during the welcome time in a worship service. It's not just being polite or friendly. It's about deep and honest relationships where we know other people and they know us. In these relationships, others spur us on to know the Lord, and we them. We walk the road of life together, and become mature in Christ in a mutual sharing of gifts, talents, resources, and love.

Scripture gives us ingredients for real relationships. In light of Scripture, here are four ways we build a church that's hard to leave.

1. We are honest with each other.

Honesty is the foundation of real relationships. Without honesty, solid relationships in marriage, in the family, or with friends have no chance of forming. People sometimes belittle the practice of foyer small talk, where we run into each other on Sunday morning and one person says, "How are you?" and the other person says, "Fine." I don't belittle it, because it's a key that opens a door; it's a necessary part of forming real relationships. But foyer small talk can't be all there is. We must commit to working past that to forming relationships of substance and depth. Husbands and wives need relationships with others of their gender. Our kids need Christian friends who help to fill the hole reserved for human relationship. If bad company corrupts good morals, then we must strategically connect our families with those who will encourage good morals. We do this by taking the time to connect.

Listen to these powerful words from Colossians 3:9–10: "Do not lie to each other, since you have taken off your old self with its practices and have put on the new self, which is being renewed in knowledge in the image of its Creator."

Ephesians 4:25 says, "Therefore each of you must put off falsehood and speak truthfully to your neighbor, for we are all members of one body."

Practicing honesty is a difficult command to obey. What does it mean to tell the truth or put off falsehood? How can we get to know people well enough to be transparent about our own lives and to invite them to join us in developing a deeper relationship based on honesty? We must be truthful about who we are and where we are on our spiritual journey. Once the surface small talk has opened the door, we need to intentionally go deeper. We might purposely become part of groups where trust is intentionally fostered. Then, when someone asks, "How are you doing?" we can give a fuller, honest answer, one that's beyond small talk or the normal, expected response. Sometimes someone knows us so well that they don't even need to ask—they know how we're doing by looking into our eyes.

It's our responsibility to do all we can to lead our families to places where real relationships can be built. We join with God's family to build spiritual ropes that help keep us upright and strong in this crazy culture.

How do we create a church that's hard to leave? We encourage and model honesty in our relationships. We tell other people the truth.

2. We confess our sins to one another.

When we become aware of personal sin, we might think all that's required is confession to God. And theologically, this is part of the truth. Christ alone forgives our sins and opens our way to relationship with Him. Our sins that separate us from God are forgiven by God. Romans 4:5 is clear that God "justifies the ungodly," and Psalm 32:2 says, "Blessed is the one whose sin the LORD does not count against them." God is the unique and sole justifier of sinners.

Yet James 5:16 gives us this powerful—even surprising—directive: "Therefore confess your sins to each other and pray for each other that you may be healed. The prayer of a righteous person is powerful and effective." Why would James instruct us to confess our sins to one another and pray for one another, when only God forgives sin?

It's because grace is lived out in practical community with other believers. How many times have we confessed a sin before God but still not felt forgiven? We might pray and pray and pray, but it's when we get with other people and confess our sins before God together that we truly grasp that we are forgiven. Others are able to minister to us by helping us unpack what Scripture tells us about God's response to confession. People can pray for us and give godly counsel about dealing with the consequences of our sin. People can counter the accusing voice of the enemy, who will tell us that our feelings, rather than God's Word, are true. It's when we bring our struggles into the light and get help with defeating a besetting sin that we can conquer the behaviors that have controlled us. Our lives are lived out in community, and in this manner we become spiritually mature.

Are our spiritual leaders modeling honesty and transparency and building the expectation that Christians will regularly confess their sins to one another? This should not happen during the public weekend worship services, unless the sin has affected the entire body. Rather, confession should take place one-on-one or within smaller groups, where trust is established and real friendships formed. When I confess my sins to other people, I don't confess every sin to everyone in the church. The more intimate the sin, the fewer people I share it with.

How do we build a church that's hard to leave? We confess our sins to each other, and we pray for each other to be forgiven. Also . . .

3. We carry each other's burdens.

When we struggle with a problem, there's always a temptation to clam up, to want to solve the problem entirely on our own. Maybe we feel embarrassed about the problem. Or maybe we've grown up thinking we're supposed to figure things out all by ourselves. Maybe the church we went to in the past did it that way—no one shared, everyone relied on themselves and pretended everything was fine. Look—we get help on everything these days. We take our car to a mechanic. We get help with our taxes. Why would we think we can handle our emotional and spiritual problems alone?

Galatians 6:2 spells it out: "Carry each other's burdens, and in this way you will fulfill the law of Christ." This verse implies both strength and gentleness. Yes, it takes work to carry each other's burdens. Burdens are heavy. Ultimately, we help people place those burdens at the foot of the cross. We pray for people, we roll up our sleeves and help, we enter into the messiness of real relationships.

As we help others with their burdens, we need to be gentle in words and actions. Gentleness is needed because it's easy to get upset when people close to us mess up. We must choose: ignore their burdens and feel guilty, or get involved at personal cost. We believers often want to live a happy, pain-free life with few inconveniences. But we have been given grace through Christ, and it's our responsibility to extend this grace to others. Our goal is to become Christlike, and we are never more like Christ than when we forgive and extend grace. If a person falls down, it's not our place to berate them for falling; rather, "Two are better than one, because they have a good return for their labor: if either of them falls down, one can help the other up" (Eccles. 4:9–10).

4. We celebrate together.

As believers, we not only go through trials together, but we celebrate the successes as well. Over the years it has been such an encouragement to me when others notice the good things about me that I often miss because I am a perfectionist. For them to then share the way God has used me to bless them is so affirming. It's like a voice from heaven that says, "Good job, Jim." I am reminded that God has shaped me for something important and is working in my life when sometimes I just don't see how it is making a difference when I try.

This affirmation, this celebration of the good things, has affected my family as well. Because my kids have seen how others play a part in my life, they feel like a part of a bigger family. Many of these same people have allowed me to celebrate the accomplishments in their lives as well, whether it's placing in state as a wrestler, or graduating from high school, or leading their first small group, or celebrating a milestone in their marriage. We take time to celebrate our children's major accomplishments, and we celebrate those of others in our spiritual family. These celebrations are memories that forge friendships and family, laying the foundation for more of the same kind of living as our children grow older.

How do we build a church that's hard to leave? By carrying each other's burdens, building honest relational ropes within Christ's body that hold us and our children fast in a stormy world. We learn to rely on community. We don't try to go it alone. We walk the road together.

The Incredible Power of Forgiveness

Your personal experience may make you doubt that churches can become places of forgiveness, healing, and grace. People often come to our church who have been hurt by Christians or churches elsewhere. I'm sure that people also get wounded and leave our church. Because we are imperfect people, forgiven in Jesus but imperfect in the present, we have to deal with conflict and misunderstandings. We must constantly work to heal while simultaneously working to prevent harm.

Churches are not perfect places. Sin creeps in and gains footholds, and the devil loves to exploit every weakness in our sinful nature. People misunderstand each other because they have broken filters. We must also constantly work to safeguard our churches from divisive people—wolves who come in, seeking to destroy what God is trying to accomplish. The Bible itself offers examples of betrayal, of broken trust. Jesus was a perfect leader and created a small group of twelve disciples, and Jesus led them perfectly. But the small group itself was not perfect. The disciples were often slow to understand Christ's vision. Jesus asked them to pray with Him in the Garden of Gethsemane, but they could not stay awake, even for a little while. Peter denied Jesus three times. Judas betrayed Jesus to the point of death.

Likewise, the apostle Paul wrote of feelings of abandonment by the very people he had mentored. "Do your best to come to me quickly," Paul wrote to Timothy, "for Demas, because he loved this world, has deserted me and has gone to Thessalonica" (2 Tim. 4:10). We are not told exactly what Demas did, or how exactly he loved the world, yet we can see the pain the situation caused Paul. He writes of another hurtful incident: "Alexander the metalworker did me a great deal of harm. The Lord will repay him for what he has done. You too should be on your guard against him, because he strongly opposed our message. At my first defense, no one came to my support, but everyone deserted me. May it not be held against them" (2 Tim. 4:14–16).

That last phrase is key: "May it not be held against them." That speaks of the incredible power of forgiveness. Certainly when we are creating churches that are hard to leave, we must learn what forgiveness is, and model this forgiveness as it comes from Christ to us. Forgiveness is seldom easy. Yet if you've been hurt by a church or by people in the church, then please know that forgiveness is the ultimate answer. We can try to ignore the pain. We can try to forget the memories. We can try to keep ourselves so busy that we have no time to think. We can listen to our culture and blame our past and present problems on those who have hurt us. Or we can go completely off course, into rebellion.

Yet forgiveness is the ultimate answer. Forgiveness removes the power of bitterness and pain. It's far easier to teach about forgiveness than it is to practice it. We seldom want to forgive people who have hurt us, but forgive we must.

When I (Bill) was nine, I accepted Christ as my Savior, and even then I wanted to be in the ministry someday. One year later I took a step in the opposite direction when a youth pastor molested me. It happened upstairs in my pastor uncle and aunt's home, and when I came downstairs the morning after the experience, I heard my parents and aunt and uncle laughing. Looking back, I'm sure they weren't laughing at me, nor at what had happened to me, but as a ten-year-old, I drew the faulty conclusion that I could not trust my parents, pastors, or the church. And God didn't protect me, so I thought He didn't care and I could not trust Him either.

For the next ten years I was a sick and lost lamb, running from family, church, and God, and I fell deeper into isolation and sin. Out of this hurt, I felt not just lonely but alone. My hurts felt like they wouldn't heal, and I was so vulnerable to other sins and to negative influences. I had no confidence. I desperately longed for other people's approval. I sought to find someone who would love me and someone I could trust.

One day at age twenty-one, I was sitting on a rock overlooking the ocean in Santa Cruz, California. I watched other people having fun together, but fun and relationships seemed beyond my reach. I had tried to carry my burdens alone, but I couldn't. I tried to fix myself, but I only made it worse. I tried to find someone to love me, but they left me. Ever since I was ten years old, I had contemplated suicide, but I had finally come to the end of any hope. I decided to walk to a nearby railroad track, wait for the next train to come along, and step in front of it. That's how miserable I was.

As I watched the waves coming to the shore, I thought, *Those waves have been coming to the shore for a long time. God has been reaching out to me for a long time too.* I didn't hear His voice, but I knew the thoughts were God's truth, and I prayed, "God, I don't know if You're even there, but if You are, I sure do need help." That was the beginning of healing and of my journey to forgive others and forgive myself.

God began to do a work in me and to change my life. The next year I met Bobbi. We dated and then married. As

I experienced Bobbi's love, her forgiveness for my failures, and her trust in me, I began to believe God loved me too. That enabled me to begin restoring relationships with my parents and siblings. Mentors and wise counselors came into my life. A man named Fred Masteller became my mentor. His wonderful wife, Carol, and their four children were all walking with the Lord. Fred showed me what it was like to be a husband and father. He walked the road with me for years and years and still is, at age eighty-seven.

But as I grew in so many areas, I still had a dirty little secret. I had never told anyone of the molestation and I had not forgiven the molester. Keeping that secret opened the door to a pattern in my life of being critical and unforgiving.

One day, at age fifty-six, I was teaching a Bible lesson on forgiving others, and the very same youth minister who had molested me forty-six years earlier walked into the back of the auditorium and sat down. As an adult I had tried to find him, but he had changed his name and I quit trying. But even after forty-six years I recognized him. I immediately felt chills and began to shake. I felt like that hurt and confused ten-year-old again.

I managed to finish my lesson, and I was grateful that he slipped away before I could talk with him. During the following week, God was at work in my heart. I knew I needed to confront this man, and ultimately forgive him, because I was called by Christ to do so. I didn't want to. I wrestled with what it really means to forgive. I wanted this man to say he was sorry first. I wanted to hear if he had repented and whether he had let God change his life. I wanted him to promise to change his behavior and turn himself in to the police, and only then would I forgive him.

Yet two verses came to mind, again and again:

- "And forgive us our sins, just as we have forgiven those who have sinned against us. . . . If you forgive those who sin against you, your heavenly Father will forgive you. But if you refuse to forgive others, your Father will not forgive your sins." (Matt. 6:12, 14–15 NLT)
- "Forgive others, and you will be forgiven. Give, and you will receive. Your gift will return to you in full—pressed down, shaken together to make room for more, running over, and poured into your lap. The amount you give will determine the amount you get back." (Luke 6:37–38 NLT)

It wasn't wrong for me to want to see justice done, to see him locked up to protect other children, or to want him to change his behavior. Yet the Holy Spirit was convicting me that even though God had forgiven me, I had not really experienced the full blessing of His forgiveness because I was unforgiving.

I came to the conclusion that *my part*, my forgiving him, was not dependent on *his part*, repenting and changing. I needed the Lord to change my heart and give me the ability to forgive that man. My unwillingness to hold out forgiveness was keeping me captive and hurting me. As I fought the battle inside, the Lord kept convicting me of my sin and reminding me of His own righteousness. I wanted to give that man what he deserved rather than what he needed. I have to confess that was one of the longest weeks of my life.

But then I thought, *What if the Lord gave me what I deserved rather than what I needed?* I had said the words "I forgive him" about this man thousands of times, and yet

I couldn't forget. Then I remembered that forgiving does not remove the memory.

I concluded that in forgiving others, we may never forget; we simply choose to turn them over to the Lord for His judgment of their sin (John 16:7–8), and we move forward. In my mind, I continued to protest, *If I forgive him, then he will get away with it!* But I knew that wasn't true. Forgiveness would allow me to turn him over to God for punishment. It would no longer be my responsibility to hate him or punish him. I needed to remember that he could fool me, but he could never fool God. God would know just how to judge him.

I thought, *But I don't feel like forgiving!* Then I remembered that forgiveness isn't a feeling. It's a decision, a choice. I argued, "I'm tired of this! How often do I have to forgive?" But I knew that I would have to *choose* to forgive every time I remembered for the rest of my life.

Finally I needed to face the ramifications of forgiving him. I thought, *If I forgive, then am I going to have to let him back into my life? Does forgiveness mean giving him a second chance to hurt me, my children, my grandchildren, or my church?* Then I remembered that love and forgiveness are given unconditionally, but trust is earned. I remembered that

- I cannot include as my brother those God has not included, and I cannot exclude those God has included.
- forgiving the person who wronged me may or may not include letting him back into my life. Forgiving him and turning him over to God for judgment does not mean I have to place that person in a position to hurt my family or church. And I don't need to be friends with a man just because I've forgiven him.

- forgiving him does not mean he does not need to go to jail for what he has done. I can forgive but still allow people to face the natural consequences for their actions.

Here's how the experience concluded. I wrote the following in my journal, and I share it to show how, although a church can hurt, a church can also heal. If you've been hurt by a church, apply the principles of forgiveness to your own situation.

From my journal:

I am fifty-six years old. The man who molested me when I was ten attended Bible study last week. He had changed his name, but I recognized him. I had known if I ever saw him again I would have to confront him and so I've prayed, looked at God's Word, talked to Bobbi and my mentors, and prayed some more. I talked to the key leaders of the church. I knew that facing him would be difficult and I would need their love and support.

He attended again tonight and I insisted that he meet with me privately. With my wife and the leaders watching from a distance, I walked up to him and said, "I need to see you in private." I then led him to the end of the hall. I had thought about it for 46 years. I'd prayed about it for 25 years. What does the Lord want me to feel? What does God want me to say?

Arriving at the end of the hall I said, "I have needed to talk to you ever since you molested me when I was a small boy. I need you to know how your selfish action affected my total life and took away my childhood." He looked shocked at my words.

I said, "The morning after you molested me, I heard my parents and aunt and uncle laughing. In my childish and confused emotional condition, I thought they knew what you had done and were laughing about it. In that moment, the Bill Putman who had existed died. I'd been a happy kid before that. I had accepted the Lord and wanted to be a minister. But in that one terrible experience, I no longer trusted God because He knew what you had done to me and didn't stop you. At that moment I thought my parents knew, so I couldn't trust them to protect me. I thought because you and my uncle were ministers, I could no longer trust the church."

I explained to him that from that moment, I stepped away from my faith, my family, and I began to wonder, "Am I a homosexual? What did that man see in my life that he would do that to me? God must not care about me."

I continued, "Your act upon my life started me down a path that nearly killed me." I went on to tell him how I started searching for who I am, and I fell into pornography, promiscuity, and deceit. I explained how I withdrew into myself and away from my family, failed in school, and how I finally came to the place of trying to kill myself. I paused, and he said nothing. I said, "What you did to me killed me . . . killed the person I was. I have grown to realize I can't blame you for the many bad decisions I made after that, but your act set me up for failure and took away my innocence and childhood."

He said, "I don't remember doing that."

I quietly said, "That's a lie."

He said, "I didn't know what I did would have that effect upon you."

I said, "That too is a lie. You knew what you were doing was a sin, and in your selfishness, you chose to do it anyway." I asked, "Have you molested others?" He said nothing. I took a deep breath and said, "I have been rescued by the Lord, but I wonder how many other children you have sinned against."

Not looking me in the eye, he said, "Will you forgive me?"

I said, "I forgave you many years ago and thousands of times since. In order to survive I turned you over to the Lord for judgment. I know that Satan used you. I don't hate you or want you to go to hell, but I do know that unless you gain forgiveness from the Lord, and unless you have repented and changed your behavior, then you will face God's wrath." I said, "What is your present relationship to the Lord?"

He said, "I'm trying."

I said, "Are you still in the homosexual lifestyle?" He didn't answer, but just looked at the floor. I said, "Will you let me pray with you?"

He said, "Yes."

With great difficulty I put my hand on his shoulder and prayed, "Lord, thank You for being with me through all the pain of my childhood. Thank You for forgiving me for the terrible choices that I've made." I took a deep breath and said, "Father, I don't want this man to go to hell. Would You please help him truly repent for his sins and let You forgive him and change him? Father, I would like him to be in heaven."

When I finished praying, I said, "I have forgiven you, but as the minister of the church, I don't trust you. Unless you have truly repented, and are ready to change your behavior, I cannot have you attend this church again." He said nothing. I asked him to turn around and look down the hallway. I said, "Those men are the leaders of this church, and I have told them what you did to me and what I'm saying to you." He said nothing. I told him, if he truly wanted to be right with God, God would help me and the church leaders to help restore him. I concluded by saying he could attend this church only IF he had truly repented and would accept help and counsel in being restored to God. He said nothing and left.

I returned to my wife and the leaders absolutely exhausted. Bobbi and God held onto me tightly that night.

What Will You Do?

A church that young people don't want to leave faces the hard stuff and deals with it. A church where a young person can feel safe follows both grace and the law of the land. For example, a church can require criminal background checks

Bill's Notes for Deeper Reflection
Five Truths about Forgiveness

Only when we have God's forgiveness for our own sins and the Holy Spirit to empower us can we forgive others. Forgiveness is not easy. It's not simply difficult; without God it's downright impossible! We can't give away what we don't have. We can't truly forgive anyone until we are truly forgiven.

1. Forgiveness is a choice. We are commanded to forgive, but it is a conscious act of our will, not something we usually *feel* like doing.
2. I need God's forgiveness every time I sin, and I need God's help in forgiving those who have sinned against me. Forgiveness must take place moment by moment, day by day.
3. Forgiveness doesn't mean forgetting. We often remember the hurt and at times feel the hurt. We must choose to forgive *every time* we remember, or we become victims all over again.
4. Forgiveness is a lifelong process. The deeper the wound, the longer the denial, the more you hate the person who hurt you, the longer the process of forgiveness will take.
5. My forgiving someone doesn't erase their consequences. Everyone affected by the sin will have consequences, memories, and fears to deal with. I can forgive and turn them over to God for judgment, but everyone who was hurt will have to live with the consequences the sin brings. But also know that God can take the greatest wounds and bring about eternal good with them. He can help us handle the pain and even diminish it over time. He can use our scars for His glory and for other people's good to bring healing to their hurt.

for anyone dealing with youth and children, can be careful about little protections such as signing children in and out of the nursery, and can stand ready to face harder issues. Church leaders inform themselves on the legal requirements and act responsibly in reporting to the police when needed, such as in cases of child abuse or molestation. Leaders in churches where people don't want to leave and prodigals feel welcome to return never sweep sin under the rug; they deal honestly with it and even take strong action where discipline is needed. However, they also have a strong restoration process in place for people who repent and want to change.

How do we build churches that are hard to leave?

We follow the Lord, who helps us grow to be like Him, and we join others in living life together. We never build perfect churches, unfortunately, but we can build churches that are characterized by honesty, confessing our sins to one another, forgiving each other as Christ forgives us, and bearing each other's burdens.

From my (Bill's) journal two days later, I wrote this prayer:

Lord, thank You for helping me. In my flesh, one minute I wanted to run from that man and in the next minute I wanted to beat him to within an inch of his life. Thank You for lessening the hurt and hate and giving me pity for him. Lord, only You know the ways Satan used that man to hurt me and try to end my life and hopes. Lord, only You know the others he has hurt, but I thank You for being with me all those years and for helping me face the man who started me down an ugly path to self-destruction. I love You, Lord.

PART 2

THE ORDEAL

4

When the Prodigal Wants to Leave

I (Jim) have been a prodigal, and I've had a prodigal son. I have worked with thousands of prodigals and walked with many parents through the pain of watching children take the prodigal path. I want to tell you some of my personal story—both about me and my son—and offer some principles for what you can do for the prodigal in your life. I know that when you're in the middle of it, life can be so emotionally charged that it's hard to apply principles. You're in the grip of pain and the terror of possible consequences for both your straying child and the rest of the suffering family. But my encouragement is to give yourself grace. Walk prayerfully through each day. Enlist wise counselors who can help you step back and reason through your emotions and circumstances.

When I was around eight years old, my cousin's parents were going through a divorce, and my parents graciously allowed him to live with us as his parents worked things out. The darkness he introduced to our house affected me and some of my younger sisters and set into motion behaviors that nearly destroyed us all. I experienced shame and guilt from that chaos, and as I grew older, I tried to cover up my wounds with sports, alcohol, drugs, and immoral behavior. Mostly I felt like a big zero, always needing to prove myself.

I remember feeling anger all the time and fear that I would be found out and could never be forgiven. I was angry that my dad was a pastor and was gone or busy so much of the time. He made very little money, so it seemed like we had less than everyone else. I felt my parents were getting used up from ministering to people who didn't appreciate it. My parents were totally committed to Jesus and their pastoral ministry, and my dad didn't have good time boundaries back then. The phone rang often, and he always answered it, even during dinner, and it was always somebody from the church with some urgent concern that Dad needed to attend to. I was an active child who pushed the boundaries, so much of my experience with others in the church was disciplinary. During those years, I would have told you that I was a Christian, but I was very far from God. I had prayed to receive Christ and been baptized, but as I grew up I had zero spiritual fruit in my life. I had many questions but got few answers to scratch my intellectual itch. In school and in friendships, I struggled because we had moved so many times during my relationship-forming years. The only time I felt confident was on a sports field or wrestling mat—or when I had a good buzz from whatever I was using.

When I went to college, several professors attacked Christianity from day one. I figured they were well educated and knew what they were talking about, so I let myself be convinced by their lies. It eased my guilt, because I had always felt like if there was a God, I had surely failed Him. But if there was no God, then I didn't need to worry about that anymore. I was seriously struggling with alcohol by then. My first year of college, I held a full wrestling scholarship but was redshirted, so I had absolutely no excuses left for *not* drinking. I plunged into an out-of-control lifestyle. I drank away all my money, expressed frustration with my fists, and sought physical relationships with women wherever. I became a practical atheist. If someone asked me if I believed in God, I answered no.

My parents told me I was wrong but kept loving me anyway. When my dad and I talked, it often led to arguments, so he began to send me letters— the only way he could finish a thought without me disagreeing with him. He wrote about the things he wished he'd done differently in parenting me, and how he'd always love me no matter what. I knew I embarrassed my parents, but in a way they embarrassed me too. I put up walls between us, but they never allowed me to burn the bridges, making it clear there was always a pathway home. I often humiliated my parents, but I didn't care. When my anger was out of control, I purposely set out to be a public menace just to embarrass the pastor.

At one point I drank away my money and had little for food. As a last option, I asked my dad and mom for money. They agreed if I would read some literature they would send me. We had argued about whether there was a God and I had scoffed at the idea. My father had told me that there were many theist scientists, and I saw this as an oxymoron.

I had refused to even look into it. Now my father had the way to pressure me to look into why an intelligent person could believe in a God. Because I was hungry and broke, I agreed. The study led me to concede that there was a God. When my father saw the change in my opinion, he sent me Josh McDowell's *Evidence That Demands a Verdict*. The concept of the book was intriguing to me. I was studying to get my teaching degree in history, so to study religion based on history seemed like the next best step. Still unwilling to believe that the true religion could be Christianity, I took the historical criteria from Josh's book and began to study world religions. I reasoned that if God had stepped into history in a tangible way, then it would be historically provable. I understood that if God existed, He would have the ability to do miracles, but there would be real historical evidence to prove a miracle. Historically, you don't accept a book as truth merely because it's old, but verify it by certain criteria. I studied Buddhism first because I liked the idea that I was a god (eventually one with god) and that there isn't a hell—merely reincarnation. Later I studied Mormonism and several other religions, but still, much to my parents' chagrin, I refused to look at Christianity. I just didn't want to go there. Finally in frustration, my dad called me a coward for not studying Christianity, and this caused a huge argument. At this point I decided to look into Jesus but only to prove that my dad was a fool.

At the same time, the wrestling season was over and my drinking was accelerating. I got into serious trouble at a college event, and the school leaders decided to cancel my scholarship. My wrestling coach stepped in to get me one more chance. Alcohol and marijuana were destroying my grades and wrestling career, my relationships with my family members, and my friendships. My coach informed me that if I didn't get some help during the summer break, I was done. I had always said I could quit using whenever I wanted, but now it was clear that I had lost control. I had to take some steps forward, so I sheepishly asked my parents if I could come home. My dad said yes, but he set boundaries this time. He wrote out a contract and made us both sign it, then copied the contract fifty times because he was pretty sure I'd throw it away or say it didn't exist. I was unpredictable about my partying and drinking and fighting, so my parents needed to protect the rest of the family. They borrowed my uncle's trailer and put it in the front yard for me to stay in. I had to check in every night with them to prove I was not drinking, I had to hold a job, and I had to go to church every weekend. I had to continue to read and study the historicity of Christianity, as well as be connected to a support group my coach had helped me connect with.

As I continued to study, I became increasingly aware that Christianity was different from all other religions I had studied. There was real evidence, and I was finding it harder and harder to rebut it. I was now realizing that God existed and that the only historically provable religion in the world was Christianity. But this did not make me feel better because I did not understand the gospel. I felt there was no way the God of the Bible would forgive me after all I had done. My relationship with my parents had grown and healed in many ways because they had never cut me off. I began to feel guilt and shame that I had sought so hard to escape. I began to feel such sorrow for what I had done to my parents and my sisters, and my behavior slowly began to change.

I was working a side job laying irrigation pipe, and Dad decided to push the issue of my relationship with God. Up to that point, I had not shared my change of mind or my understanding of what it all meant. One day just before I left for work, he followed me to my car and asked if I had come to any conclusions about Jesus. I opened up just a bit to say, yes, He was the Son of God. Dad asked if I was ready to give my life to the Lord. I got emotional (which I did not see coming) and said there was no way God was going to forgive me. Dad began to speak, but I quickly got into the car to hide my emotions. I left for work, and when I came home, I saw that Dad had left the Bible open on my bed to Ephesians 2:1–10.

> As for you, you were dead in your transgressions and sins, in which you used to live when you followed the ways of this world and of the ruler of the kingdom of the air, the spirit who is now at work in those who are disobedient. All of us also lived among them at one time, gratifying the cravings of our flesh and following its desires and thoughts.
>
> Like the rest, we were by nature deserving of wrath. But because of his great love for us, God, who is rich in mercy, made us alive with Christ even when we were dead in transgressions—it is by grace you have been saved. And God raised us up with Christ and seated us with him in the heavenly realms in Christ Jesus, in order that in the coming ages he might show the incomparable riches of his grace, expressed in his kindness to us in Christ Jesus.
>
> For it is by grace you have been saved, through faith—and this is not from yourselves, it is the gift of God—not by works, so that no one can boast. For we are God's handiwork, created in Christ Jesus to do good works, which God prepared in advance for us to do.

I got the point. We are saved by God's grace. It doesn't matter how far we stray. The apostle Paul, under Holy Spirit inspiration, had written those words. At one point in his life, Paul had actually killed Christians. So I concluded that if Paul could be saved, then God could certainly save me if I was ready to surrender my pride and shame and guilt.

That day sparked many conversations with Dad, and finally I decided it was time to give my life to the Lord for good. Dad baptized me in a canal, with just my mother and sisters there. It was an amazing experience, and I knew that many people had been praying for me to come home.

I knew I was saved then—truly saved—but there was more work to be done. In the next few years I was able to get back to college and wrestle as well. I met Lori, a Christian who would become my wife, and between Jesus, her, and my parents, I was surrounded. However I refused to be a part of a church, though my father would prod me about it continually. I read my Bible and would listen to my dad preach when I was home, but would often tell him that it was Jesus and me, and he and Mom would be my church. As a pastor's kid, I felt too wounded from my parents' experiences with church. One day, after a couple of years of shrugging him off and avoiding the argument, my dad called me. He said, "Jim, I have a question for you. I have an issue and I need some outside wisdom. There's a family in the church that wants to get to know me more. They want me to come to dinner. But it's funny—they don't want Mom to come. They said they don't care for her and would just like to get to know me."

I was incredulous—furious! The idea that somebody could say this to my parents! I was baffled too—my mom might be the kindest woman in the world. How could they like my dad and not her? It made no sense. My first response was, "And you wonder why I don't want anything to do with the church?" But my dad calmed me down and said, "Jim, this is exactly what you are doing with the church, the bride of Christ. You say you want Jesus, but you can't stand His church." That analogy really blew my mind. I got his point and started going to church.

About a year later I had moved to Boise and was going to a church there. I didn't like it and was frustrated with the church again—seemingly perfect people, pretending, not really doing anything. I shared this with my dad, and he said, "Jim, a healthy lake has water going in and water going out. If water only comes in, then soon the lake floods and kills everything around it. If water only goes out, then soon it dries up. You have had water flowing into your life for a long time now, but no water is going out. Church isn't just something you attend, it's something you are a part of. Read 1 Corinthians 12, Romans 12, and Ephesians 4. Pray about it, then go serve somewhere."

So I read and prayed. Two weeks later the pastor called me out of the blue and said, "Jim, we have four high school kids in our church. You and Lori are the youngest couple attending, so would you be interested in doing a Bible study with them?" I didn't know what to do, so I called my dad. He said, "It sounds like the Lord answered your prayer. Now get in the game!"

I didn't know how to do a Bible study with a group. I'd been truly saved for only a year and a half. But my dad worked with me. He said, "Look, just read a Bible story and then share a few minutes on how this has applied to you. Ask them some questions, and if they ask you questions that you don't know how to answer, say you don't know but you'll find out. Then you can call me and we will work through it." My dad discipled me all the way from when I turned my life over to the Lord to where I'd found my place in the body of Christ and could use my gifts and abilities in the church.

From that place of volunteer service, five kids became ten, ten became fifty. I eventually became a full-time youth pastor. Then I was a part of a church plant that grew exponentially—Real Life Ministries, where I'm the lead pastor today.

Christian's Story

My father, Bill, became a prodigal because of woundedness. I (Jim) became a prodigal mostly out of rebellion. And then came my own son, Christian. Lori and I have three sons—Christian, Jesse, and Will. Christian is the oldest.

When Christian was young, a female babysitter molested him. That started him down a road of shame and guilt. He has some learning disabilities and often struggled in school, so he felt dumb, which isn't true. He also inherited the rebellious sin nature that we all have. At age thirteen, he started doing drugs with some of his wrestling friends and was addicted by the time he was a sophomore in high school. He was pretty much out of control, and I didn't even let him go to youth group, because all he did there was try to sell drugs and pursue girls. It was bad enough that he was so far from Jesus—I couldn't let him lead other kids astray too. By his junior year he'd already gotten DUIs, been in jail, and moved on to the worst kind of drugs. In his senior year he got a girl pregnant, and she had the baby. Then Christian quit school.

One night he overdosed on drugs and was in a coma. As soon as he got out of the hospital, he ran right back to drugs and his so-called friends. He'd sometimes go missing and be found days later without a shirt and shoes, walking at night in the snow. He became paranoid and his sanity was slipping.

He landed in jail once again, and we made a deal with his probation officer to send him to a three-month rehab center. We had to sell our house to pay for it, but it was worth it just to sleep through the night knowing we would not get a tragic call from a police officer saying he had killed himself or someone else.

I was going through the wringer during all of this. In one of Christian's worst seasons, he'd come into our house, high and belligerent and verbally lashing out at Lori, calling her names. I lost it. I actually knocked him out. When he got up, he ran from our house and my wife wept for hours. My other boys had witnessed this and were so confused. My middle son, Jesse, was so angry. When I tried to talk to him, he said, "You have told us over and over to walk away from a fight—never give yourself to anger—but you did it." I was broken—he was right. I immediately wrote a letter to our elders, saying I had decided to resign and went to a meeting to give it to them. After hearing what I had done, they tore up my resignation letter and said as a church they loved us and were going to walk through this with us as a family. They said, "No way—you don't resign from family. You have helped us in different ways when we were wrong or hurting, and we will help you." The elders and staff stepped up to take some of my responsibilities. They had known of our situation and prayed with us often—now they were there to help carry our burdens. They sent Lori and me to a great counselor. Lori tended toward enabling and I tended toward rules and consequences—we just couldn't get on the same page without help in this situation. With the help of Jesus through Christian counseling professionals and our church family, we made wise decisions that would eventually set the stage for changes that Christian could only make on his own. We were able to work through what was our part, what was God's part, and what was our son's part. We could not do God's part or Christian's, but by doing ours, we could rest in the knowledge that our God was involved even when we couldn't see it.

When he got out of rehab, he was sober and we got him back in school. He stayed in school for about two months, then started using again—and this time the drugs were the worst of the worst. He got arrested again and went to jail. We sent him to a Teen Challenge program in Oregon. He was there for only three days and they told him to pack his bags and dropped him off at a homeless shelter.

That was the lowest of the low for us. I was on a mission trip to Mexico with our son Will when Christian went into the shelter. Lori and I had decided beforehand that whatever happened with Christian, we wouldn't bail him out this time. Christian called Lori and begged her to drive the eight hours to come get him, but we said no. That was particularly difficult for Lori. She called our small group and asked them to help her by coming over and taking her keys so she would not go get him. I called him from Mexico, and he said, "Dad, you have to come and get me because these people are crazy in this shelter." It was so hard to tell him no—we had exhausted our money and our energy. He was affecting our younger sons and had lured one into trying drugs. I said, "Christian, you need to get used to living with crazy people, because you will have to live with them under bridges for the rest of your life unless you decide to change." I told him he could show his heart change by staying rather than calling friends to pick him up—he could start going to a recovery program right there.

Every day was a battle for Lori and me. It killed us that our son was on the street by himself in a strange area with many who were corrupt or mentally ill. We begged God to protect our son from himself and others. We prayed, "Lord, do what it takes but please keep him alive." Often, well-meaning Christians would question how we could do such a thing. Our wise counsel helped us know that sometimes you have to let someone hit bottom before they decide to stop their rebellion. Sure enough, it started to work, slowly, with many ups and downs. For four months we agonized through his slow recovery. He started walking to AA programs multiple times every day all over town. Every week he would ask if he could come home, but we would say not yet. Despite much progress, he found a way to reconnect with some of his friends back home. A former girlfriend went and got him (without our consent or knowledge) and brought him back to our hometown. We would not let him live with us because we were frustrated that he had not listened to our counsel and we did not believe he was ready. We had to protect our other boys and our sanity. Sure enough, he was sober for a little while, then started using again.

I'm going to tell you more of this story in bits and pieces, but in summary, Christian eventually got straightened out and sober and turned his life over to the Lord. He's now in full-time pastoral ministry.

Passing the Right Baton

What do you do (or not do) as parents when a child starts living like a prodigal?

The sad fact is that too many parents don't pay attention to what's happening with their children along the way, because they are too busy chasing the world (being prodigals themselves). Or maybe they focus energy on wrong things. I know so many parents who devote themselves to their kids' sports but not to their kids' faith. They keep their eyes on their abilities to succeed in school or some other good-but-not-great endeavor, but completely miss that the most important thing is their heart toward Jesus. These parents often wait until it's too late and the child has become a full-blown prodigal. That's why we encourage parents to pay attention and head things off at the pass.

Our goal as Christian parents is to help create the *fullest experience of the faith* possible for our children. Surely we must give them Bible knowledge. We must also help them find their place of service in the body of Christ—God's team. But there is more. This is so important: we must help them develop many strong Christian relationships with other believers. As I have already stated, relationships are like ropes that help hold us fast to the family of God. These aren't casual friendships or surface interactions. They're open and honest relationships where believers walk the road together.

I encourage Christian parents to help their children develop many godly relationships, at church, in youth group, at school, through camp, and even at other youth groups. Help your children develop friendships with godly family members and neighbors. Make it hard for them to leave the faith because to do so would mean leaving a spiritual family that has meant the world to them. Often kids are able to leave the church easily because they don't know anyone there to begin with. *Their parents do not model real relationships because they bounce from church to church or attend only occasionally.* Without real relationships they don't experience all the "one another's" in Scripture, such as forgiving one another, bearing with one another, confessing to one another, carrying one another's burdens. With no experience of a working faith, kids have little trouble abandoning it.

But many parents do many right things, and their child becomes a prodigal anyway. There is no foolproof way to prevent a child from going astray. I've seen families where all the children are raised the same way. One child turns out fine but another rebels. We are all sinners (Rom. 3:23) and a child's free will comes into play (1:18–32). Remember that the prodigal son had a very good father and lived in an ideal household, yet he strayed. A child chooses for himself whether to follow the Lord or to stray. There's brokenness inside every person that causes us to say, "I want what I want—even if it's not good for me or it's harmful to others."

Sometimes, too, people become prodigals because they have grasped only a form of the faith. They have not experienced true faith and were never discipled to maturity. They might say they love God, might have memorized Scripture verses as a kid and have perfect Sunday school attendance, or appear morally upstanding, or go on mission trips, or stay off drugs, or remain a virgin until marriage—but none of these means the teen is actually saved and walking with the Lord wholeheartedly. Christian parents can help kids experience the true faith. This may not guarantee a good result, but it gives kids clear-eyed choices. If a child has not experienced the true faith, then they may think they've tried Christianity and it didn't work.

So many things can knock a young person off course. It might be a dating relationship gone wrong, or alcohol, or drugs, or an influential university professor who attacks Christ, or their parents' divorce, or some sort of abuse, or some sort of pain, or the wrong kind of friends who lead a person astray. Ultimately, the problem is always a problem of the heart. As parents, we are quick to attack the symptom, not the root cause. Our teen is out drinking, so we attack drinking, but it's only a symptom of something else. Maybe he wants acceptance from friends. Or she's drinking to cope with some sort of hurt. We must get to the real reason our prodigal is rebelling. Remember, we can only do our part. We cannot do God's part or theirs.

Help for Parents of a Prodigal

From the story of the prodigal son in Luke 15:11–31, we can develop principles to help with our own prodigal children. Here is some practical help for parents of a prodigal:

1. Be aware of your child's heart.

The good father in the story was aware of the prodigal son's condition, as well as the older brother's hardness of heart. In both cases his children were able to approach him and tell him anything, and if they didn't talk, then he approached them to talk. In both cases the father heard his kids but also shared his heart. To the one he showed that his son mattered more than his own possessions or good name. He said and did nothing to make the younger son feel he could never come back. With the older son, the father heard his anger but reaffirmed his love. He also reminded him that he should be happy because his brother who was dead was alive again.

It's important for us as parents to develop a sense of awareness with our children. We can't give you every detail of what to say or how to respond to each individual child (that's where you pray and seek wise counsel). But we can encourage you to develop a spiritually mature family where open and honest talks are the norm.

Regularly seek to have conversations with your children. Maybe around the dinner table. Maybe at the end of the day before bed. Maybe when you're driving in the car. Within the context of a loving relationship, ask open-ended questions about their friends, school, social media use, hobbies, events, interests. Don't grill them. Don't lecture. It's about seeing how they're doing. You are inviting them to open up. Listen, and listen closely. Listen for what isn't said as much as for what is. Spend much more time listening than talking.

2. Leave the door open, but protect the family.

Remember, under Mosaic law, the father of the prodigal son actually had the right to kill his rebellious child (Deut. 21:18–21). At the very least he had the right to say, "You're not getting anything from me." But the good father didn't take that kind of action. He left the door open for the prodigal to return, and this is almost always the best course of action to take with a prodigal.

The two-pronged key with your prodigal is to be strong in your God-honoring boundaries but maintain the relationship. Invite your prodigal to dinner, although it might be an uncomfortable time. Invite prodigals home for Christmas and Thanksgiving. Attend graduation and marriage ceremonies, even though your heart may be breaking at their lost potential or about who your prodigal is marrying. Let your prodigal know that he or she is always welcome to come home.

Notice how the good father set boundaries. For instance, he didn't give the lost son both his share and that of his brother too. We must try to protect our other children, because their lives are affected by the rebellious sibling. They may feel that the prodigal is taking up too much of Mom and Dad's time or ruining the happy family dynamic they used to enjoy. All our children need a safe place to unpack their hurts. This is where relational ropes in the family of God can help. The prodigal's siblings may see your pain and not want to add to it, but they can share and unpack their feelings with others in the body of Christ whom they've learned to trust. Without the ability to be honest and bring the hurts to light, the devil can cause a bitter root to grow up that can destroy them.

My dad set boundaries for me. My alcohol use as a college student negatively influenced my younger sisters, which is one reason I needed to not be at home at all for a while and later live in a trailer in our front yard temporarily when I came home.

3. Respond in love; be willing to let go.

The way the good father responded—and *didn't* respond—revealed something of his depth. He could have responded in anger, fear, bitterness, or humiliation, but instead he responded in confidence, security, and love. In essence, he said to his lost son, "My possessions and name are not as important to me as you are. I love you. If you want to go, then I will let you go." As a free-will agent, the only way the boy can learn is to get what he thinks he wants.

Are we willing to let our prodigals be prodigals? We can't coerce anybody into righteousness. If someone wants to live in sin, then we need to respect the free-will choices they make. By "respect" I don't mean we need to like or endorse their choices, but we respond as the prodigal father did, in love. Sometimes they need to leave the home—to suffer natural consequences for their actions. We must allow the consequences without our fear or anger driving us to sin.

Certainly there are age-appropriate boundaries. For instance, if a twelve-year-old insists on leaving home, then that can't be allowed. But if the rebellion escalates, maybe there are alternative courses of action. If the situation is bad enough, maybe a relative or someone in the church family can take in our prodigal for a while. He or she may even need to go to juvenile detention. Yes, sometimes we must call the police because our child is breaking the law and could hurt themselves or others. My wife and I had to remember that God can work even in jail. He is not bound by bars.

The good father didn't negotiate right and wrong. He didn't welcome overt sin into his house. If his son wanted to be a prodigal, then the father let him go, but he didn't welcome prodigal actions or attitudes into his home. He didn't give him his inheritance to spend at home. That would be like Eli in the Old Testament who allowed his sons to defile God's sacrifices rather than fire them from their jobs. God punished Eli for placing his sons above God.

4. Trust that God is working; constantly look for the prodigal's return.

In the prodigal son's story, the famine was no coincidence. The pig farmer was no coincidence. God orchestrates people and circumstances to work in our prodigal's life, and our call is to trust that God is working, even while our prodigal is far away. Romans 5:8 says, "God demonstrates his own love for us in this: While we were still sinners, Christ died for us." God is working, even if we don't see tangible fruit of that work right away.

Because he believed God was working, the good father constantly looked for the prodigal son to return. He believed the son would one day come to his senses and come home. I mentioned that when I was at my worst, my father wrote letters, constantly telling me how much he loved me, how he forgave me, and that I could always come home. I couldn't party at home, but I was always welcome.

In my own son's life, when Christian was at his worst, I gave him a phone and texted him every day to tell him I loved him. He responded in various ways, sometimes blaming me, sometimes cursing at me. But I kept texting, telling him I loved him, that when he was ready to come home based on certain conditions, he was always welcome. I believed this was the right approach because the Lord does the same kind of thing. God has sent us His Word as a text from heaven throughout history, saying, *Come home. Why are you still there? I love you.*

5. Expect some suffering.

The good father allowed his son to feel hunger and loneliness, shame, disgust, and embarrassment. The good father allowed his son to squander his money, live wildly, eventually hit rock bottom, and eat with pigs. This was undoubtedly painful for the good father, as well as the son. But the good father did this so the world could teach his son the truth that he'd refused to see at home.

Certainly we will want to have many conversations with our prodigals, to give warnings, to help our children press the fast-forward button and imagine the results of their actions

Bill's Notes for Deeper Reflection
Fourteen Powerful Ways to Deal with a Prodigal

1. **Don't assume their responsibility. (You are only responsible for the one you can change—yourself.)**

   Ezekiel 18:20 "The person who sins will die. The son will not bear the punishment for the father's iniquity, nor will the father bear the punishment for the son's iniquity; the righteousness of the righteous will be upon himself, and the wickedness of the wicked will be upon himself" (NASB).

2. **Don't cover up for them.**

   Ephesians 4:15, 25 "But speaking the truth in love, we are to grow up in all aspects into Him who is the head, even Christ. . . . Therefore, laying aside falsehood, speak truth, each one of you with his neighbor, for we are members of one another" (NASB).

3. **Always work to restore them.**

   Galatians 6:1–2 "Brethren, even if anyone is caught in any trespass, you who are spiritual, restore such a one in a spirit of gentleness; each one looking to yourself, so that you too will not be tempted. Bear one another's burdens, and thereby fulfill the law of Christ" (NASB).

4. **Don't gossip about them.**

   Proverbs 18:8 "The words of a whisperer are like dainty morsels, and they go down into the innermost parts of the body" (NASB).

   Proverbs 17:9 "He who conceals a transgression seeks love, but he who repeats a matter separates intimate friends" (NASB).

5. **Ask for advice and seek help.**

   Proverbs 11:14 "Where there is no guidance the people fall, but in abundance of counselors there is victory" (NASB).

   Romans 15:14 "And concerning you, my brethren, I myself also am convinced that you yourselves are full of goodness, filled with all knowledge, and able also to admonish one another" (NASB).

6. **Use the total resources of the church and home.**

   Ephesians 4:15–16 ". . . Christ, from whom the whole body, being fitted and held together by that which every joint supplies, according to the proper working of each individual part, causes the growth of the body for the building up of itself in love" (NASB).

7. Keep up your own daily devotions and prayer.

Psalm 1:1–3 "How blessed is the man who does not walk in the counsel of the wicked, nor stand in the path of sinners, nor sit in the seat of scoffers! But his delight is in the law of the LORD. And in His law he meditates day and night. He will be like a tree firmly planted by streams of water, which yields its fruit in its season, and its leaf does not wither; and in whatever he does he prospers" (NASB).

1 Thessalonians 5:17–18 "Pray without ceasing; in everything give thanks; for this is God's will for you in Christ Jesus" (NASB).

8. Be light and salt before this person.

Matthew 5:13–14, 16 "You are the salt of the earth. . . . You are the light of the world. A city set on a hill cannot be hidden. . . . Let your light shine before men in such a way that they may see your good works and glorify your Father who is in heaven" (NASB).

9. Don't return evil for evil.

1 Peter 3:8–9 "All of you be harmonious, sympathetic, brotherly, kindhearted, and humble in spirit; not returning evil for evil or insult for insult, but giving a blessing instead; for you were called for the very purpose that you might inherit a blessing" (NASB).

10. Always trust in the Lord.

Matthew 6:34 "So do not worry about tomorrow; for tomorrow will care for itself. Each day has enough trouble of its own" (NASB).

11. Remember to seek first God's will.

Matthew 6:33 "But seek first His kingdom and His righteousness, and all these things will be added to you" (NASB).

12. Don't be afraid to take a stand for truth, even if it separates you from others.

Joshua 24:15 "If it is disagreeable in your sight to serve the LORD, choose for yourselves today whom you will serve: whether the gods which your fathers served which were beyond the River, or the gods of the Amorites in whose land you are living; but as for me and my house, we will serve the LORD" (NASB).

13. Don't be afraid to let them leave if they refuse to serve God.

Luke 15:11–32 (A son chooses to leave his father's home.)

1 Corinthians 7:15 (An unbelieving mate chooses to leave.) "If the unbelieving one leaves, let him leave; the brother or the sister is not under bondage in such cases, but God has called us to peace" (NASB).

> **14. Always bring your burdens to the Lord.**
>   **Matthew 11:28-30** "Come to Me, all who are weary and heavy-laden, and I will give you rest. Take My yoke upon you and learn from Me, for I am gentle and humble in heart, and you will find rest for your souls. For My yoke is easy and My burden is light" (NASB).

if they keep going this way. But if these conversations and wise counsel don't work, then we acknowledge that prodigal living will bring suffering. If that's what it takes for our prodigals to come home, then so be it.

We can have peace even if this sounds like the opposite of love. It's not. Love sometimes allows people to suffer, not as punishment, but to act as a teacher to bring people to their senses.

It's All Worth It

Really, the whole Bible shows us God the Father responding to His prodigal children. In 2 Corinthians 5:18–21, we see how we're reconciled to God through Christ and given this message of reconciliation. Paul says, "We implore you on Christ's behalf: Be reconciled to God" (v. 20). Indeed, this is the whole message of the cross. "God made him who had no sin to be sin for us, so that in him we might become the righteousness of God" (v. 21).

In 1 John 1:9, we see, if we go astray, how Jesus is faithful and just to forgive us and to cleanse us from all unrighteousness. These are the actions of our homecoming. We are all prodigals in our sin, but when we repent, when we at last come to our senses, then Jesus welcomes us home with open arms. We are forgiven and cleansed.

I (Bill) remember when Jim was living as a prodigal; not yet at rock bottom, he was wrestling out in Chicago in the national championships. There was a lot of tension between us and Jim, but we wanted to celebrate his accomplishments— and celebrate him—even in the midst of his rebellion. On my pastor's salary, we didn't have money to travel from the West Coast to Chicago, but we made it a priority, borrowed money, and I made the trip. We wanted Jim to know we supported him.

When I got there, he spotted me, ran across three mats, picked me up, and gave me a huge hug. And I thought to myself, *This is love. I will never stop loving my son, ever. It's all worth it.*

5

The Pain of Exposure

This is a true story, although names are changed. We see the patterns in this story being repeated throughout churches today—and we want to address this issue head on.

A concerned father—let's call him Fred—came to talk to the youth pastor at his church, whom we'll call Joe. Fred has a son we'll call Ryan, who had seemingly walked with the Lord throughout high school. But Ryan was now in college and making poor choices: not going to church, not plugging into any college-age ministries around town, out many evenings with friends, smoking pot and drinking. And mostly, Ryan's heart was far from the Lord. Essentially, Ryan was living as a prodigal.

Fred was angry with Youth Pastor Joe. He blamed him for pouring too much time into the high school ministry and not enough time into the college group. Fred wanted Joe to create better church programs that would captivate Ryan and kids like him. Fred insisted that the reason Ryan wasn't walking with the Lord was because Youth Pastor Joe "hadn't done his job." Fred told Joe to shape up, and if he didn't, then Fred would go to the elders to get Joe fired.

Youth Pastor Joe listened to Fred, heard him out thoroughly. Then Joe tried to "solve the problem." Joe explained about limited staffing resources. It was true that the high school department received more attention than the college department, but there were reasons. Joe trained volunteers for both areas, who developed relationships with the students, but there was a limited number of volunteers.

Joe described several ministry-related solutions for Ryan, where he'd already tried to direct Ryan. Most college-age students left their small town and went elsewhere to school. The high school group had about forty, but the college group had only four or five. So Joe encouraged college-age students toward various college-related ministries in town, including InterVarsity and Fellowship of Christian Athletes. But Ryan was not interested.

Fred wasn't interested in listening to the youth pastor. He wanted his son walking with the Lord—now! He grew angry with Joe again, pointed his finger at him, and told him, "Do your job."

The meeting ended poorly.

So, what went wrong—both from the youth pastor's perspective and from the father's?

Solutions Come in Three Parts

Having a prodigal in our lives can expose us—in a good way—although the exposure doesn't always feel beneficial at the start. *Exposure* in this sense means that the crisis reveals deeper things in our own lives. We might not be prodigals ourselves, but ultimately, the crisis shows where we may have gone off the rails or developed false beliefs that need to be challenged. God may allow or ordain circumstances that expose our attitudes and beliefs, revealing our deep need for God's ongoing help.

When my son Christian was still in high school and going through his rebellious season, I (Jim) was senior pastor of Real Life Ministries, as I am now. Our town, Post Falls, has a population of about 35,000, and our church has about 6,000 people, so we have a fairly large presence in town. Christian was known in high school, in the community, by the police, and by the church. Christian embarrassed himself and my wife and me publicly on many occasions. It was painful. His DUI and arrests for that and other things put us all in a poor light in our little community.

Once, I went to the school after Christian was arrested to find him handcuffed, walking down the hallway with policemen on either side of him. It was lunchtime so everyone was in the lunch room as we walked through and I recognized many faces. I was absolutely humiliated. All I could do was fall in step behind as they led him through the cafeteria and halls to the police car. When your children rebel, it exposes all sorts of vulnerabilities in you where you need the grace of God. It can prompt a sanctifying process in your life. While I followed my son in handcuffs, a thought rushed at me, as if Jesus spoke to my heart: *Jim, when I was crucified, they stripped me down and walked me through the middle of a street, and I hung on a cross naked for you. You can love your son the same way. Go walk through this with your son.* And so I did.

When a prodigal leaves home (or church), chaos and tension can enter a family. It's much like a hurricane sweeping through. The prodigal leaves and others are left to clean up the mess. Some people try to ignore the problem, some become angry and blame others. Some give in to depression, and in grief over the broken relationships, they withdraw and isolate themselves. They may consider leaving their family or church. For me, though I had been sober for many years, the temptation to retreat into alcohol again was the strongest it had ever been. Some people are swept away by guilt and regret—they dwell on what they wish they'd done or hadn't done. If only they'd been a better parent or friend or ministry leader, then the prodigal wouldn't have done this or that. Some people live in constant fear—they don't know how it will turn out and don't feel safe to share their disappointment with themselves, their spouses, and even with God. Some obsess over possible explanations for the problems. Some become bitter and hardened.

When Christian was going through his difficult season, Lori and I disagreed on how to parent him and sometimes argued about it. The crisis exposed weaknesses in our marriage and in us as individuals. In Lori's case, as I have said, she would tell you today that she was an enabler. She loved Christian so much that she was willing to do anything for him, even inadvertently helping him continue in his sin. In my case, I was too harsh. Often, my first reaction toward Christian was disappointed anger. Lori and I weren't on the same page. We were desperate, and our desperation exposed just how much we needed God. I was angry at God, ashamed of myself, angry at my wife. I functioned in fear, and I urgently needed to do business with God.

For me personally, it was about needing to let God speak to my heart where I was wrong, to show me where I had made and continued to make mistakes, and let Him meet me in my sin. I needed to allow God to work on my anger and fears. Lori feared that if we laid down the law too strongly, then Christian would run and never return. In youth ministry, she had seen how some fathers had laid down the law. She watched how the resulting separation affected the mother as well, as there was little reconciliation even years later, and this terrified her. Lori believed if we just did the right thing (whatever that was), it would cause Christian to change—to do the right thing too. I had gotten to the point that I believed nothing we did would cause Christian to want to stop (we had tried and failed), so we had to force him to do the right thing. My fear for Christian was that if we didn't stop this sin trajectory, he would destroy his life forever. So I swung the pendulum too far in the direction of force.

In the example at the start of this chapter, both the father and youth pastor cared about the student. But they had differing solutions on how to handle the problem, and in a sense both missed the real solution. In the situation of any prodigal, there are three levels of responsibility, and it's helpful to distinguish who is responsible for what.

God's Part

"God's part" refers to things that only God can do. God creates, commands, communicates, empowers, assigns responsibility, forgives, shepherds, and restores.

God draws people to Himself in a variety of ways, and every person must agree with Him and no longer conform to the world (Rom. 12:2). It is ultimately God's work in partnership with a person's will that transforms. Thank the Lord that, because God knows what it will take, He can work through circumstances to bring a person to Himself. It's a great comfort to know that while your prodigal can run from you, they can never run from God.

Many times in the crisis with our son Jim, Bobbi and I (Bill) were left empty. We would come to the end of ourselves and lay huddled in bed together and let God hold us. In our marriage and parenting there were times when our everything was not enough. We failed. All we could do was cry to the Lord to hold us together and help us rebuild our home. We discovered that when our cord of two frayed and broke, the Lord became our third cord (Eccles. 4:12). We discovered that when we were afraid and had no answers, God was faithful.

My Part

"My part" refers to the responsibility of the person who cares for the prodigal. In the case of the first story, this would be the father and the youth pastor, because both cared. They cannot do God's part or the prodigal's part, but they each can do their own. Yes, there are things we can do to help prodigals. We can pray for them, counsel them, listen to them, maintain our relationship (in whatever form the prodigal will allow), forgive them, and encourage them to get involved in disciple-making churches.

As parents and spiritual leaders, we choose whether to follow the Lord ourselves, and then we choose whether to do our part to raise children in the discipline and instruction of the Lord. We choose to pray for God's wisdom. Then we choose to trust the Lord and wait for an opportunity.

But my part is always limited. I cannot save a prodigal myself. If a prodigal truly wants to turn away from the Lord and is determined to do so, then no amount of my effort will prevent that. When I know what my part is and isn't, then that actually frees me from guilt. It lets me rest in the work of the Lord.

We were a mess. Jim was in full rebellion, our oldest daughter was in Bible college, another daughter was suffering from abuse we didn't know about, our thirteen-year-old was nearly forgotten. Just three weeks after the full-term death of our first grandchild, I was a guest on *Focus on the Family*.

Dr. James Dobson asked me, "Bill, you must be a mature man to let the world know about this and not be overcome with guilt and self-condemnation, all the things that parents wallow in. The natural thing is to say, 'I'm a failure; it's my fault,' and try to conceal it or deal with it defensively. How did you escape all of that?"

I said, "Well, I haven't. My son and I had conflict and I felt all those emotions. I blamed myself and wondered what I did wrong. I had sense enough to go to a Christian psychologist and begin to work through those difficulties. Bobbi and I read *Parents in Pain* by John White. He gave me permission in this book to not accept all the guilt and responsibility."

Bobbi and I knew we had taught our children right and wrong, and we had been in relationship with our next-to-youngest daughter. When she announced, "I'm pregnant, and I'm so sorry." I felt sadness, remorse, and disappointment, but I did not honestly feel guilty. (The full program aired multiple years on Father's Day as "Daddy, I'm Pregnant.")

Why the difference between our reactions to our rebellious prodigal and our repentant prodigal? Our daughter had let God do His part to save her, and let us (parents, sisters, grandparents, and church) do our part to restore her. With Jim we were doing our part, but Jim rejected help.

Their Part

"Their part" refers to the responsibility of the prodigal. Ultimately, the prodigal is responsible for their own actions. Every individual must choose whether to trust God and love and obey Him (Rom. 1:21–28). If the prodigal is deciding not to follow the Lord, that's their choice.

Similarly, if the prodigal wants to return to the Lord, then their responsibility is to humble themselves, pray, seek the face of the Lord, and confess their sins (2 Chron. 7:14). The prodigal must undertake to renew their mind and to grow spiritually (Rom. 6:19). The prodigal should also try to restore relationships that they damaged on their way to a far country.

Yes, the prodigal has responsibility in this process—a lot of responsibility. They make decisions for themselves. They will ultimately stand before the judgment seat of Christ and be held accountable for their actions, good or bad (2 Cor. 5:10).

Watch Out for the Trap

Father Fred and Youth Pastor Joe needed to sort out who was responsible for what. Fred and Joe could do only so much. If Ryan was truly choosing to walk away from the Lord, then Ryan was responsible for that decision.

But there's something larger happening in that conversation. The father had not understood the whole problem and was insisting that Joe take responsibility for things that were out of his control. If you give yourself the wrong job description as a parent or leader, you'll wind up with a broken heart.

We who care deeply for prodigals can easily find ourselves trapped in the false belief that if we only try harder at the right things, then we can make up for another person's failure to trust the Lord. We might believe that if we are a good enough parent, then we will be able to save our children. If we are a good enough friend or ministry leader, then the people in our sphere of influence will never walk away from the Lord. If we try harder, read more, pray more, do more, teach better, create better programs, lead better Bible studies, then people won't "go prodigal."

That sets up a false if/then scenario, because it ignores that the solution is not all up to us. The Lord does His part, and then each individual is responsible for their actions. Certainly, there's a call for biblical mindfulness and excellence in parenting, friendship, and leadership. Our job (our part) is to do our best to lead our kids to the real Jesus. Often we have not revealed the real Jesus; therefore, people reject a false one. So we must showcase Jesus by being in relationship with Him, abiding in Him, bearing fruit, humbly asking forgiveness when we fall short. But let's grasp this: it's not all up to us.

In parenting we often claim Proverbs 22:6 as a promise: "Train up a child in the way he should go, even when he is old he will not depart from it" (NASB).

I (Bill) blindly trusted that if I raised my children right, it would guarantee that good outcome. I claimed this verse again and again when my children were going astray. The verse puzzled me as much as it gave me hope. I saw others in the church who had raised their children well, but the kids had been straying for years and showed no signs of returning to the Lord. I had suffered through funerals of children raised in Christian homes—children who died of drug overdoses or as avowed atheists. I saw other parents who'd raised their children poorly, not "in the Lord." They hadn't tried half as hard as I had to be a good parent. Yet they had great children. Had God misled me and not kept His promise?

I know a dear minister's wife who raised her children well. She's in her nineties now, and her oldest child, in his late sixties, is still not saved. She told me, "Well, I still have hope. You know what the Scripture says . . . ," and she quoted Proverbs 22:6.

The question for us is whether this verse offers a guarantee. Does Scripture actually promise that if we raise our children properly, in spite of their free will and our parenting imperfections, then our children have no choice but to come back to those teachings when they are older?

A Closer Look at God's Promise

If we insist on claiming Proverbs 22:6 as a blanket promise for parents, then we have a problem. God the Father was a perfect Father to Adam and Eve in the Garden of Eden. Yet Adam and Eve chose to rebel against the Father. Claiming the verse as a formula—that if followed perfectly, leads to the perfect result—is a mistake. In the first place, we can't follow our end of it perfectly; we cannot raise up our children in the way that they should go in absolute perfection. Second, it disregards the fact that our children have a free will.

Let's go back to one of the original parenting commands in Deuteronomy 6:4–9:

Hear, O Israel: The LORD our God, the LORD is one. Love the LORD your God with all your heart and with all your soul and with all your strength. These commandments that I give you today are to be on your hearts. Impress them on your children. Talk about them when you sit at home and when you walk along the road, when you lie down and when you get up. Tie them as symbols on your hands and bind them on your foreheads. Write them on the doorframes of your houses and on your gates.

That passage instructs us to observe, obey, and keep the commandments of God, to let no person or thing take God's place, and to love God wholly. We're to impress God's commandments on our children, to teach them in every scenario of daily living. And we're to wear God's teachings on our bodies and place them on the walls of our homes.

But as we know from Romans 7:7 and other passages, the full function of God's commandments is to convict us of sin. God gave His commandments for us to follow, knowing we would never be able to follow them completely. Our knowledge of God's law brings us to the end of ourselves and lets us know we're sinners in need of a Savior.

For most of us, the reality of Deuteronomy 6:5 is more like this:

We love the Lord our God with **most** of our hearts and **some** of our soul and **part** of our strength.

I confess that's how I operate. I must have tried a thousand different methods to be a good parent, and succeeded often, but still failed an awful lot. We all play the "if only" game, repeating, "If only I had listened more, shown more affection, disciplined more consistently, spent more time, prayed more, kept my mouth shut more, been more forgiving," and on and on. I never got up one morning and thought, *I'll be a lousy dad today*, but in reality I often was.

I arrived home during a time of deep trouble and found my wife and daughter having a good cry. Our daughter said, "I wish I were ten years old again." Out of my mouth came words that have changed me for a lifetime: "You can't go back, but because of Christ, you can start over."

The wonder of God's grace is that in all our imperfections, He imparts to us salvation when we trust in the finished work of Christ. As we continue to trust, we can start over again and again.

So, what is God saying in Proverbs 22:6? It is a general principle more than a specific promise. Taking in the full counsel of God, we see that God always allows people to have free choice. That means if we train our children in godliness, if we prepare our children when they are young to be disciples of Jesus who love, serve, and obey Him, if we continually pray for our children and set Scripture before them so it finds its way into their minds and hearts, then generally our children will do okay. But the proverb is not an absolute guarantee, because self-will and deliberate disobedience on our part as well as our child's part must be factored into the equation.

Let's make this more practical. If our children could become spiritually mature Christians by our parenting alone, then they wouldn't need Jesus to be their Savior.

The test of our homes isn't whether our children become spiritually mature Christians, but whether we ourselves have loved, trusted, and obeyed the Lord. The test of our children's lives will be whether they listened to truth and chose to follow the Lord themselves.

Children are never ours. They are on loan from the Lord. They are God's potential children first, and it has never solely been up to us to raise up our children. God uses parents, extended families, other Christians, churches, friends, schools, books and other resources, and even the government and police to raise children to maturity.

The bottom line is, when everything else fails, including parents, God still loves our children. He loves them even more than we do. We cannot follow God's commands perfectly, but His grace is perfect for us. So our job is to partner with God in His mission to raise children who become wholehearted followers of Christ. Our job as ministry leaders is to partner with God in His mission to raise up people who become wholehearted followers of Christ.

A Closer Look at God Himself

Back to our story of Fred the Father and Joe the Youth Pastor. Something huge is at stake in Fred and Joe's conversation about the concern they show for Ryan: God's character and the way He works in time and space. Fred and Joe are coming to grips with who God is and how He acts.

Both Fred and Joe have been praying that Ryan will return to his senses, return to the Lord, and become a wholehearted disciple of Jesus Christ. They are praying for a restored family and loving relationships. Yet God has already shown us in Scripture that He will not force Ryan to follow Him. However, God knows if there is something that will bring Ryan to his senses and when in the future that might be. We need to trust that He will do His part when the timing is right. He is also able to teach us to trust Him during the waiting game and to use all the mistakes our loved one is making right now for some future good. It may seem like God is not answering our prayers, at least right now. So Fred and Joe must come to grips with all of this.

When people we love walk away from the Lord, we ask God for help. Often we beg Him to answer our prayers. Perhaps we try bargaining with God by making promises. Maybe we think, *If God truly loved me, then He would never let this happen.* We confess our sins, thinking that our sin is the reason God is "bringing judgment" and allowing our loved one to walk away. We wait for God to show up, but it seems like He doesn't answer us, so we begin to doubt God ourselves. God isn't answering our prayers the way we want, so we grow angry or despondent with God. The devil has a heyday with this, accusing us of failures and poor decisions, so that we feel we cannot go to God with our requests anymore. Or the enemy whispers that there is no God at all. I met recently with a man who told me he had prayed for years as his son spiraled out of control with drugs and depression. When his son committed suicide, the father said if God existed, He would never have stood by and let that happen.

Here's what we need to learn about God: if we have a wrong view of God, or an incomplete view of how God acts, then when sorrow comes into our lives, the sorrow will crush us instead of drawing us closer to God. Remember, God didn't create puppets who are forced to do what He wants. He gives every person free will so we can choose to accept His love and love Him back or choose to reject His love. He creates us to be full of life and joy, but we can make choices that hurt and even destroy us. God is sovereign. But being a perfect Father, He waits, He respects people's individual decisions, He never forces or imposes His will on people.

Jesus gave us a picture of His heart when people freely reject Him: "O Jerusalem, Jerusalem, the city that kills the prophets and stones those who are sent to it! How often would I have gathered your children together as a hen gathers her brood under her wings, and you were not willing!" (Luke 13:34 ESV).

What that all boils down to is that sometimes God answers our prayers by giving us what we ask for, but other times He says "no" or "wait." God chooses to answer prayers the way He sees fit, according to what He sees from His perspective. He is able to see how everything plays out and knows how every decision affects every other decision with everyone involved. Our call is not to understand the reasons of God but to trust the character of God. God is always good, all the time.

Here's the big warning for all of us: if we are angry or frustrated or irritated or impatient that our child or a friend has turned away from the Lord, and if we have asked God to restore that person to Himself, and if the person is still not walking with the Lord, then our continuing anger, frustration, irritation, or impatience is directed to God Himself.

We prayed, but God didn't answer that prayer with "yes."

So, why are we not at rest?

It's because we don't fully trust God to do His part. But let's be assured, if we pray to our heavenly Father, He hears. He knows the number of hairs on our heads. He keeps track of our tears in His bottle. He knows our heart and He loves our prodigal more than we do. Our role is to do the part that He asks us to do. And then to trust Him to do His part.

Our Help Comes from the Lord

Trusting God with our prodigals is perhaps one of the hardest lessons we will ever face. It's one thing to know the truth of God's goodness in our minds. It's another thing to place our hearts in God's hands when people we love are in harm's way.

That's when we need to run to God's own goodness. Run to Him, not with demands in hand. Run only in faith. Run, believing that God is ultimately a loving God who hears.

Bill's Notes for Deeper Reflection

Truths about Prodigals

(Heb. 4:12–16; Luke 15:11–31)

Public prodigals first face the battle for the mind:

> They look out from the home, drawn to what they don't have.
> They become discontented.
> They become self-centered.
> They lust for what they don't have, and plan how to get it.
> They plan how to remove whatever stands in the way.
> They suppress belief in God and focus on getting what they want.

Public prodigals next face the battle for their behaviors:

> They don't honor God or parents, or give them thanks.
> They act out their rejection of God and family values.
> They act out their sinful thoughts.

Next public prodigals face the battle for their habits:

> They suppress belief in God and worship what pleases self.
> They exchange the truth of God for a lie.
> They know God will judge but sin anyway and encourage others to sin.
> They face consequences of their choices.
> They lose relationships with family and others who care.
> They lose what they value most.

I (Bill) found that it's so easy to want to vent at this point. The stress of worrying for our prodigals boils up inside, and we can't help but release that stress somewhere. It's okay to vent to the right people who will love us enough to listen and point us back to faith. We are meant to live in community with other believers, and if trusted people are in your life

Prodigals lose good friends to find false friends.

Prodigals, losing so much, become jealous of pigs or beggars.

Prodigals know if they go back, they face issues of trust, relationships, forgiveness, and debt.

Public prodigals are convicted of their own sin:

They know they have sinned against God.

They know they have sinned against family.

They may try to cover their deep sense of loss with more sin.

Private prodigals are like the older brother. They stay at home but may be bitter and jealous about the love and attention given to the public prodigals, both while they are missing and when they return.

All prodigals can repent:

They can have a change of mind that leads to change of behavior.

If their parents are godly, they may go home.

If they come from a godly church, they may return.

If not, the heavenly Father offers to change their lives and work with them.

All prodigals can change their minds and choose to act:

As long as there is life and Christ's forgiveness, they can come to their senses.

Prodigals are able to come home.

Prodigals can choose to confess their sin.

No prodigal is hopeless.

who love you as you vent, then this is part of encouraging one another in love (1 Thess. 5:11) and carrying one another's burdens (Gal. 6:2).

I (Jim) found that good Christian friends helped me process even when they were clueless about what to do. They listened as I vented—loving me without judgment. I also discovered that I was dealing with things differently than Lori. During that time, we went to Mark Cornelius, who was not only an amazing professional counselor but a mature Christian who helped us individually work through things that not even a good friend could unpack. He asked me questions no one else asked and helped me refocus my thoughts in a God-honoring way.

Very practically, I (Bill) recommend that you not make important decisions when you feel out of control. There were many nights during the "crazy teenage period" when Bobbi and I fell into bed too exhausted even to sleep. Our temptation was to take out our anger on each other. My sweetest memories of those difficult years were of reaching out to take Bobbi in my arms. Many times, in tears, we'd allow the Lord to hear us, comfort and heal our hearts, and to help us remember that God was in this with us.

The best place to vent your honest emotions is to the One who handles them perfectly, the Lord Himself. God can take any emotion we throw at Him. He is big enough to handle all our fears, doubts, angers, annoyances, and griefs. As the old hymn goes, "What a privilege to carry / everything to God in prayer."[1] Everything! The Lord is there whether we feel that He is or not. He can handle it all. He invites us to boldly approach His throne of grace (Heb. 4:16), anytime and anywhere. We might be in so much pain that our prayers only sound like "groanings too deep for words," yet the Holy Spirit translates our prayers to God (Rom. 8:26 ESV). God always loves us, always accepts us, and always remains good.

Consider all the depth of emotion found in the psalms written by David, a man who did well in his youth and became a leader of the nation of Israel. But he fell into sin, had a friend murdered, became a disaster as a husband and

father, and endured one crisis after another in his family.
Hear his cry in Psalm 42:5:

> Why, my soul, are you downcast?
>   Why so disturbed within me?
> Put your hope in God,
>   for I will yet praise him,
>   my Savior and my God.

David is venting here. He's admitted his soul is downcast
and disturbed. He's discouraged, sad, annoyed, troubled,
and grieved. Yet in spite of his feelings, he remembers the
kindness of God. David puts his hope in Him.

In the midst of one crisis in our family, I (Bill) specifically remember going to the Lord and crying out in my pain and hurt,
"O Lord, help! Because I feel so helpless." And God seemed to
impress upon my heart, "Oh, Bill, let Me help by carrying you
as we go through the valley of the shadow of death."

No Easy Solutions

Let's take a closer look at our responsibility. What can we
personally do? When a child or a friend runs from the Lord,
there are no easy solutions. Some well-meaning people make
the mistake of offering pat answers, but pat answers ring
hollow. There are at least three choices we can make in our
efforts to help. Two of those choices will harm. One will help.

1. We can choose to take all the blame.

If there's a prodigal in our life, then it's easy to feel
like it's all our fault. We become overwhelmed with
our own guilt, trying to make up for our mistakes that

we think caused their actions. We feel we need to run after the rebels so we can keep them from suffering the consequences of their actions, or we become a doormat or a beggar and try to do whatever it takes to bring this person back. No. This is not the way to go.

2. We can choose to judge.

It's easy to point at the prodigal and concentrate on his failures. "It's all his fault!" we conclude. "Why does he have to ruin our family (or friendship) this way?!" When we do this, we typically withdraw from the person or erect barriers. We become angry, demanding, critical, and defensive. We fail to see the person with eyes of compassion. We fail to see ourselves robed in the character of Christ, ourselves in the role of the good father, constantly looking to the horizon, longing for the prodigal to return.

3. We can ask the Lord to change us.

The only person I can make decisions for is the guy in the mirror, the reflection looking back at me. The only person I can change is me.

The chaos brought about by a prodigal will cause tension to surface in any relationship. How I react to that tension will often expose my own sin. Many things will be out of control, but I can control one thing. I can ask the Lord to change me. Sanctify me. Continually mold me and make me more like Christ.

A Helpful Path to Take

What does this third option look like in real life? When Bobbi and I (Bill) were shipwrecked by the crises in our family—a son's rebellion, a daughter's secret hurts, another daughter's pregnancy, my own collapse—we felt like our hope was gone. The Lord helped us cling to Him and to each other in the midst of all the tension. I'm so grateful we had each other during those rough times. When one of us wanted to quit, the other looked to the Lord and helped hold on.

We committed ourselves to prayer. Abiding in Christ and washing in the Word helped us see again through God's eyes and provided strength to go on. If one of us had a bad day and the other one felt stronger, that one would simply say, "I think we should pray." And then we did.

We asked the Lord to help us always look to Him, and we asked Him to rebuild our family into a home for our children to return to; we asked Him to rebuild our church into a church ready to receive prodigals. We prayed our prodigals would see these changes as unexplainable except as God rebuilding our home and church.

We asked the Lord and our family to forgive us for sins and mistakes. We couldn't go back and erase anything or pretend it never happened. We couldn't remove our children's memories of our failures. But we could ask them to forgive us. We could ask the Lord to change our lives and begin the rebuilding.

Bobbi and I sought godly counsel and help in trying to get healthy ourselves so we could be who we needed to be before Christ. At one time when our family was falling apart, I went to our elders and tried to submit my resignation because I didn't feel healthy enough to lead the church. They said, "Bill, you have walked through crises with us. Now it's our turn to walk through yours with you." I said, "I'm sorry, guys. I have nothing to give to others right now. I can't lead, preach, or counsel." They said, "That's okay, Bill. We will step in and

help. You get healthy so you can enter back into the ministry."
That's a great example of being gracious to others!

God brought heaping amounts of grace into our lives, and little by little, the Lord healed us as individuals, as a couple, and as a family. While we were waiting for our rebels to come home, we practiced what we were learning about being gracious to each other. We loved, forgave, communicated, set boundaries, and walked with openness and humility before each other.

As we look back to the shipwreck of ourselves and our home, we have hope for anyone today. God forgave us, restored us, rebuilt us, and allowed us to start all over again. If God can heal a person, then He can heal a marriage, He can heal a family, and He can heal His church.

6

The Process of Restoration

We hear far too many stories about people hurt by the church or people who decide to rebel against the Lord and leave the church. Thank the Lord, many of these stories have happy endings.

Years ago, a staff member's wife died of cancer. He went through a grieving season and during this time had an ungodly relationship with a single woman. He eventually came to his senses and confessed it to the Lord and to his leaders on our staff. After much prayer and healing conversation, we took him out of his position for a while. We knew he needed to pay his bills, so we offered him a job as a janitor. He was humbled that we would care for him this way and took the job. We made sure he was connected in a solid group. He ended the relationship with the woman and went to counseling to work through his grief and sin issues. He had a master's degree in counseling himself, with long success in practice, so he must have been the smartest janitor we ever hired. Eventually he proved his repentance and was restored. He later married a godly woman who serves with him now in full-time ministry.

Another man in leadership at our church consistently acted arrogantly and hurt those around him. The man was confronted about his attitude but initially denied his prideful behavior. Again, after much prayerful conversation with him, we removed him from leadership. Through this experience, the Lord confirmed his insensitivity and pride. He too confessed his sin and went through a process of repentance and restoration. Time passed, and he's now back in leadership.

A man in a volunteer leadership role got into a season of intense struggle with his wife that led to public disagreements and separation. He became so frustrated with his home life that he worked too many hours, and angry outbursts became his norm. Our biggest concern was not how this appeared in public but how the couple was doing in their walk with Jesus and with one another. As much as we loved the ministry, we cared more about them personally. Often people are allowed to work publicly for the Lord when privately they are out of balance. Others are allowed to continue if problems are swept under the carpet. Still others are never pulled off the front lines when they are wounded, so they never heal. Often when facing issues like these, leaders fear that the whole ministry will unravel. But a good coach knows when to get a player off the field for their own good and the good of their team. So we lovingly asked this man to step aside from leadership until we could sort this out. In anger, he said, "I can't step out of ministry. It's the only thing that keeps me sane." Our leadership team told him no, he couldn't effectively lead people in spiritual directions with this going on. He reluctantly submitted to his spiritual authority and went through a long break to get things back on track. He and his wife received counseling, and as a church we walked them through it. Today they are both restored to positions of leadership.

Just as children in a natural family can turn away, drift, or rebel against God, children can do this in a spiritual family too. They leave the faith and are never seen again by family or church. Other prodigals stay in church and keep going through the Christian motions. They might show up each Sunday and remain involved. Some even stay in leadership positions, yet they are prodigals nevertheless.

Rebellion within a church can exhibit itself in many ways. People may become disillusioned with the church or with their concept of the Lord Himself. Such prodigals can become contentious, creating all sorts of havoc. Maybe a small group leader reveals his rebellion by refusing to do what the elders ask, and leads the group to leave the church. Maybe an associate pastor undermines the God-given leadership and causes a church split. Maybe a husband, a board member, chooses to leave his wife. Maybe a child who grew up in the youth group decides in college that they no longer believe in God.

Or prodigals can stay quiet too, invisible, hiding their hearts. This is particularly true of prodigals who are more wounded than defiant.

How do we deal with this? Perhaps you are in a position of spiritual leadership. You wonder what to do. Or perhaps you simply have a friend who fits the prodigal category and you want to help. What do we do about prodigals in the church?

Why Prodigals Go Astray

Remember, in the story of the prodigal son, there are really two prodigals. The younger brother was openly defiant and left home. The older brother was quietly defiant and stayed put. The younger brother eventually came to his senses, repented, and returned to the father. The older brother was lovingly confronted by his father, but there is no record of his repentance. We don't know if he was ever restored fully.

What about prodigals in our church? Certainly we always hope, pray, and work toward full restoration. This is so important—for us as well as them. As ministers of reconciliation (2 Cor. 5:18), we are never more like Jesus than when we reach out to people who are far from God. They need to be restored to the Father, first to fix their heart condition, and also because people need to live in the context of a restorative family. For some people, their only hope of finding that is in the church. It's in people's best interests to be restored—and that's the overall attitude with which we must approach them. We love them with the same love the Father has shown us. We love them because they are our brothers and sisters.

It's important for us to grasp how prodigals are made in the first place. What happens in a person's heart and mind and life that leads them away from Christ? We look to Scripture for the answer. All of us must contend with "the sins that so easily entangle" (Heb. 12:1–2). We all have a sinful nature that can deceive us into confusion and outright rebellion. We also have a crafty spiritual enemy who is battling against us. It's important to humbly remember, when we minister to rebels, that we are all susceptible to sin.

Yet sometimes personal sin isn't the catalyst that begins the separation process from the Lord. (As mentioned, in

Bill's life, the sin of someone else began the separation. Bill wasn't a rebellious prodigal; he was a lost or wounded one.) Psalm 13 describes the deep anguish David experienced when he felt lost and wounded:

> How long, LORD? Will you forget me forever?
>   How long will you hide your face from me?
> How long must I wrestle with my thoughts
>   and day after day have sorrow in my heart?
> How long will my enemy triumph over me? (vv.
>   1–2)

These are not easy words to hear from anyone. David describes how he wrestles with his thoughts and feels sorrow "every day." Clearly he is a man in anguish. Unlike Psalm 51, where we are specifically told that David experienced torment after he had committed adultery with Bathsheba, we aren't told what event precipitated the writing of Psalm 13. Perhaps it was again David's own sin that caused him to feel so far from God. But perhaps not. In Psalm 13:2b David wonders aloud how long his enemy will triumph over him, and that seems to be the root cause of anguish here. The ungodly prodigal King Saul chased David without cause for years, and David still had no relief. The sins of others were causing hardship in David's life. David actually loved Saul and would have wanted nothing more than to have his king and mentor come back to a relationship with God. Yet it did not happen.

This is true of many people today. Difficulty comes into their lives, and they feel like David did in Psalm 13. But unlike David, they may fail to make the connection between difficult circumstances and the need to trust God anyway.

In Psalm 13:5–6, even after David has lamented so strongly, he goes on to say,

> But I trust in your unfailing love;
>   my heart rejoices in your salvation.
> I will sing the LORD's praise,
>   for he has been good to me.

When people fail to make this connection, they often walk away from God. Maybe they were not taught how to understand the broken world we live in, or how to fight spiritually, or how to endure hard times. Maybe they were given false promises that the Christian life was a bed of roses. When people fail to see the goodness of God, even in hardships, then wounded people join the same camp as rebel prodigals.

Caring for Prodigals

We see an example of a churchgoing prodigal in 1 Corinthians 5. Paul chastises the Corinthian church because a man in the church is overtly engaged in immorality—specifically, sleeping with his father's wife. The Corinthians allowed him to bring his sinful behavior into the church, probably thinking they were being loving. They are even "proud of it," Paul notes. He asks, "Shouldn't you rather have gone into mourning and have put out of your fellowship the man who has been doing this?" (1 Cor. 5:2).

Matthew 18:15–17 outlines the procedure for dealing with sin in the church.

> If your brother or sister sins, go and point out their fault, just between the two of you. If they listen to you, you have

won them over. But if they will not listen, take one or two others along, so that "every matter may be established by the testimony of two or three witnesses." If they still refuse to listen, tell it to the church; and if they refuse to listen even to the church, treat them as you would a pagan or a tax collector.

The passage shows a four-step process of confrontation. First, go to the person humbly, lovingly, and privately. Maybe things can be resolved at that level.

If not, then second, take along one or two others to act as witnesses. This lines up with the directive in Deuteronomy 19:15 to convict a person accused of a crime only by the testimony of two or three witnesses.

If this doesn't work, then third, tell it to the "assembly." In Jesus's day, this meant the core Jewish assembly of God-fearing people. In today's context, we'd probably say the eldership of the church, who then lets the core of the church know what has happened.

Fourth, if none of this works, then treat the person as one who does not know the Lord. The person is not shunned but rather treated with compassion, as a nonbeliever is.

Luke 15:1–32 offers a clear picture of what it means to associate with sinners, who often came to listen to Jesus. He told the story of the shepherd with one hundred sheep who lost one, the story of a woman with ten coins who lost one, and the story of the prodigal son. All the lead characters in these stories went after the lost with great diligence. That's the attitude Christ displays toward lost and wandering people, inside or outside the family of God.

Still, there is an implicit boundary within the Matthew 18 directive. Sin creates barriers, and full fellowship is not possible with an unrepentant sinner. The purpose of confrontation is never to belittle or harm a person. It's to bring a person to his knees so that he will repent and escape the inevitable harm sin brings, follow Jesus wholeheartedly, and be restored to fellowship.

In my (Jim's) family, I needed to establish boundaries with my son Christian when he lived as a prodigal, because his actions were polluting others in my house. Christian was always welcome to come home, but until his repentance was complete, there were conditions. Christian influenced his young brothers who looked up to him, and I had to protect them. The same needs to be done on a church level. When a Christian brother or sister acts in willful sin and causes others to stumble, we must love them but not allow them to lead others astray. Earlier I shared that I would not allow my son Christian to go to youth group because I knew he would intentionally lead others toward sin. On the one side I wanted him to be around other Christians who might get through to him, but on the other I could not sacrifice other kids for the sake of mine.

Until repentance is complete, full fellowship isn't possible. People are welcomed to a church service and invited to meet the Lord there, but we wouldn't put an unrepentant person who is under discipline in a small group where they can influence others. Many Christians in small groups are young in the faith and need protection. Paul told the Corinthians not to associate with so-called brothers and sisters who lived as unrepentant sinners. He later said he did not mean that they should not be in contact with unbelievers, but only to cut contact with professing believers who lived in sin (1 Cor. 5:9). Paul's goal was always to reach the lost and grow and protect the believers. We certainly wouldn't put a rebellious believer in a decision-making or leadership role. Scripture gives high qualifications for leadership, and ignoring that not only dishonors the Lord but sets a tone in the whole church. When a church puts an ungodly leader up front, it tells people that the way the leader is living is okay.

What are the specific requirements for allowing a person to come back to church? It centers on this axiom: "Love and forgiveness are given freely. But trust is earned." Do you know what that means? There are no barriers to love, as Jesus showed us by dying for us while we were still sinners (Rom. 5:8). Forgiveness is likewise given freely. In Matthew 18:21–22, Peter asked Jesus how many times—*seven?*—he should forgive people. (Peter probably considered that generous, because the traditional Jewish teaching was to forgive up to three times.) But Jesus said, "I tell you, not seven times, but seventy-seven times." In other words, there is no limit on forgiveness—it's free and bountifully offered.

Yet it is still necessary to have safeguards, particularly with the issue of trust. Trust is given after the person's integrity is tested, and trust can only be established with time. Trust is conditional. The responsibility to test, rebuild, and maintain trust with a repentant prodigal is placed on those in leadership. You wouldn't leave your baby to be watched by a person who would refuse to leave a TV program if the baby cried. You would not allow an immature teenager to take your toddler on a road trip. Nor do you entrust God's family to a prodigal, not even after forgiveness is granted. Why? Because the prodigal has established a track record of sin and harmful behavior that has eroded trust.

Paul exhorts a younger pastor in 1 Timothy 5:22: "Do not be hasty in the laying on of hands, and do not share in the sins of others." The "laying on of hands" refers to giving leadership roles to people within the church. Paul instructs Timothy to make sure that trust is earned—this refers to initially putting people in leadership positions and also to reinstating people to leadership positions after they have sinned, repented, and been restored. The forgiveness is instant. The regained trust is not. When a person says he repents, we need to determine if he is just being emotional and trying to escape consequences or if the repentance is real. If so, there are degrees of restoration. A truly repentant person can be restored quickly back into fellowship, but it is a completely different matter to put him back into leadership.

We should be careful in the restoration process not to put a person in the same place where he struggled before. For instance, a married man in our church struggled with sexual sin. He was hitting on women in his small group and then had an affair with someone at work. When this was discovered, we immediately removed him from that small group situation, and when he claimed to repent, we directed him to a men's group designed by mature men who helped the sexually addicted. The man refused. He wanted to be in a mixed group again. He wanted to set the terms of his repentance rather than submit to the authority of the Lord's church. This revealed his continuing rebellion, which told us he was still a prodigal. So we went through the Matthew 18 process of confronting the man, and he was still unrepentant. In fact, we believed he was a threat. So we said, "Okay, with reluctance, you are no longer allowed to come to a church service until you repent and submit to the restoration process." After a few months he was ready for real repentance. We went through a real restoration process with him.

Another man, on our worship team, silently and secretly struggled with alcohol abuse. This went on for some time and we were unaware. Then he was in an altercation down-town where he was drunk, and the story became known. We told the man we would help him get clean and sober, if he so chose, but he needed to drop off the worship team until restoration could take place. He said no, he didn't believe he had a drinking problem, and he left the church. It wasn't long until he was playing for a different church in town. No phone call came from that church about why or how he had left us. They just saw a talented person and put him onstage. His behavior soon affected the reputation of that church in our town. We continue to pray for him, and a few key people stay in contact, but this issue is not resolved yet.

In another instance a married man acted immorally, con-fessed and repented, and went through the full restoration process. Ten years passed, and the man was nominated to be an elder. We talked to the man extensively, and to his wife, who knew him best. I asked her if she believed full repen-tance, healing, and restoration had taken place. She assured us that it had, and her husband was forgiven and restored. So we allowed this man to be in leadership again.

The process outlined in 1 Corinthians 5 seemed to work with the immoral man in the early church in Corinth, because in 2 Corinthians 2:4–16, Paul writes an apparent follow-up. The immoral man experienced the love-driven discipline of the church and felt grief over his sin. He had been handed over to Satan, to experience a world without spiritual protection—and it had worked. It's clear the man's ways were changed. Instead of urging punishment, Paul writes, "You ought to forgive and comfort him, so that he will not be overwhelmed by excessive sorrow. I urge you, therefore, to reaffirm your love for him" (2 Cor. 2:7–8). In other words, welcome the prodigal home!

Remember, the main goal in any restorative process with a prodigal is to help bring that person back to Jesus. Relationship with Jesus is always primary, but the secondary goal is restoration with the church family. What if the prodigal goes to another church? Sometimes that might be appropriate if the damage to someone within the church family is too much for them to handle seeing that person every week. But generally, true repentance plays out this way: the disciplined person works with leadership in the same church that they had hurt; these leaders are best qualified to determine the right actions to bring about restored relationship. True repentance means doing our best to make right what we have damaged. We must make things right by submitting to the same authority we rebelled against. When we sin, we are not just sinning against God but against His people in a specific local church. I know that today in the Christian world, people often bounce from church to church, with little respect for the authority of a church. But Scripture makes it clear that we are to obey the elders (spiritual parents) in the church (Heb. 13:17). Could you imagine the son in the prodigal son story saying, "I will not go back to my father but to a different father"? This would have robbed the waiting father of his joy. As churches, it's time for us to get back to the plan that God has given us for prodigal restoration.

In some cases, it might be appropriate for the restored prodigal to attend another church. But that's a decision made together for the good of all, and the original church body needs to know that the disciplined person has repented. They need to see that godly leaders who were courageous and loving enough to do what God wanted were rewarded with God's blessing—the wayward child has come home. But sometimes the decision to go to another church family may be the right thing for a restored prodigal. We might grieve and miss them, but the point is that we aren't focused on bringing a person back to a particular tradition, or denomination, or local assembly. The goal is always a relationship with Jesus and His family.

Tracking the Strays

One of my (Bill's) main jobs at Real Life Ministries is to head a team that essentially tracks down and cares for missing, lost, or prodigal people. We call it the ministry of "chasing strays," and we take our directives from Ezekiel 34, where the Lord warns Israel's shepherds what a flock looks like when shepherds have not cared for it. God declares that He is part of the restorative process Himself, and He exhorts shepherds to care for the flock, strengthen the weak, heal the sick, bind up the injured, bring back the strays, and search for the lost.

We track every church member to ensure we know on any given Sunday which of our people are worshiping with us. Everyone is asked to sign a connection card. If no card is signed, and if a person is missing longer than two weeks, then a pastor or volunteer leader contacts them. Often we know the person, so we just call to check on them. People may get off course and just need a gentle reminder that they are loved and missed. Other times there are deep problems affecting their lives. Sometimes the devil is seeking to isolate or detour them, so we pray for them and seek to help them through their issues. We encourage them to take the step of plugging into a Life Group, because merely coming to church is only part of the connection God wants for each

Bill's Notes for Deeper Reflection
Ministry of Team One

We have a group we call Team One, and their ministry is based on the story Jesus told of the man with 100 sheep where one gets lost. He leaves the 99 to seek the one and carries it home with joy.

The focus of Team One is always on that "one." The aim of Team One is to share the gospel, connect and reconnect to create biblical disciples in relational environments, train them to minister, and release them to disciple others.

Step 1: Establish a Biblical Foundation. Luke 15:3–6 and 10 is the model for an intentional ministry to reach out to missing and disconnected members, missing two weeks to six months, with a goal of restoring and reconnecting.

Step 2: Identify an Intentional Leader. The leader, under oversight and accountability of the Lord, elders, and assigned pastor, will seek to identify, equip, and oversee those enlisted in Team One.

Step 3: Build a Relational Team Environment. The team leader seeks to shepherd, equip, and disciple team members so they are able to be dis-

person. Our team contacts each person multiple times if necessary over six months. If a person is missing all that time with no response, then they're put on a nonactive list. We then send out letters from time to time or call to see if we can pray for them about anything. After a year we send a letter to let them know that we no longer consider them as our sheep but would love to have them come back and will be praying for them. If they ever return to church and want membership, then they need to go through the new-member process again. We try to get to the heart of the matter and find out what caused them to leave the first time so the matter is dealt with and doesn't surface as a problem again.

ciples who make disciples. We recruit Christians for Team One whose life experience gives them understanding of those with weak faith or who are facing physical, spiritual, marital, family, or financial crises. We also recruit those who can assist with the process of identifying, tracking, and recording discovered needs.

Step 4: Implement a Reproducible Process. The team leader continually seeks to disciple and equip team members and then to identify and apprentice additional leaders. To start, the leader will recruit up to twenty, and later more, who will be able to also contact regularly attending nonmembers. Our team continues to contact the unresponsive person up to six times, and then our team turns the person's name over to the elders. Unless the person returns, we do not continue to contact them.

Step 5: Connect the Missing and Restore the Repentant. As the missing and the rebels are found, they are offered help in being restored to the Lord and being reconnected to the church.

Step 6: Partner with Elders to Discipline and Release Unresponsive Members. Those who fail to be aligned in their loyalty to Jesus Christ, the Bible, the church's vision, mission, doctrine, strategy, and faithfulness will be turned over to the Lord and the leaders for discipline, and we pray for their restoration.

People from other churches often ask me about the specifics of this process. What do I say when I contact people? It begins by understanding the reasons why we do this. We're not trying to control people or take the role of a teacher in a classroom. We don't want them to just check a box that says they did their duty, and we don't call just to check a box that we did ours. We do this because we believe we are called to care for the Lord's children and they are called to live within the family for their own spiritual good. Again, a church is a family. It's not a casual gathering of unassociated people. We have responsibilities to each other to know and be known. The process of chasing strays is undertaken with a vision of care and concern.

The specific process I use goes like this:

1. On my first call, I'll say something like this. "Hi, this is Bill Putman from Real Life Ministries. I was just getting ready to pray for you and wondered if you have any specific prayer requests." The call is not a confrontation. The call doesn't even have an appearance of a "checkup" on a person. We're sincerely just reaching out to connect. If extensive prayer concerns surface during this phone call, then I pass along information about other ministries in the church equipped to care for people's specific needs. If the person would like to reconnect with a past leader, then we try to work out a reconnection. If they tell me that they would like to be called by one of our ministry leaders in a specific area, then I give that ministry leader the information.

2. If there's no response to two such touchstone calls, on my third call I become more assertive and direct. I say something like, "I notice you haven't been here for a while. Are you okay? I'm just concerned about you. That's all." We discover all sorts of things at this point. Somebody might have moved. Somebody might have suddenly passed away. Somebody might need to be encouraged to attend a home group. Somebody might need counseling. Often some conflict management occurs at this step. Maybe the person has been hurt or become angry at someone without resolution, and our opportunity is to be a reconciler or peacemaker.

3. If there's no response by the six-month mark, then we work to meet them in a formal exit interview. Sometimes there's still no response, but we sincerely want to know

how we could have done a better job. We're trying to uncover the nugget of the problem. If people truly want to leave, then we want to know why. If it's a sin issue on the person's part, and if it can't be resolved, then we need to be like the father of the prodigal son and let the person go, always looking down the road, waiting with arms ready to welcome them home. Please note: the person who has faced discipline is distinct from a person who has just stopped coming. After the six-month mark, if the person does not return, the contact still continues.

If a person has been through the Matthew 18 process because of sin, then we especially want them to understand that our goal is always restoration—we don't want to be harsh but loving in the process as we work to bring them back to Jesus.

This approach of not being harsh with people is so important to grasp. In the final verses of Matthew 18, Jesus tells the parable of the merciless servant. A king wanted to settle accounts with his servants. As the settlement began, a man came to him who owed him ten thousand bags of gold. The man wasn't able to pay his debt, so the king ordered the man and his family to be sold into slavery. But the servant fell on his knees and begged for mercy, so the king took pity on him, canceled the debt, and let him go.

Then the same servant turned right around and found a person who owed *him* money. The servant grabbed the man, choked him, and demanded to be paid. The man begged for mercy, but the servant said no and had him thrown into prison. The king found out about it, became angry, and had the merciless servant thrown into prison.

The point is that we all need to forgive other people in direct proportion to how we're forgiven by Christ, and keep this in mind whenever we approach prodigals. Are we merciful with them? Or do we treat them harshly? The parable of the merciless servant instructs us otherwise. This doesn't mean we can't be firm. Love often needs to be tough. But we must always approach a person in love, always be patient, always kind, never easily angered, never provoked to wrath.

Always Adopt a Gentle Tone

If the person we're contacting is struggling with sin or walking away from the Lord, then the spirit of our call must conform with the tone and directives of Galatians 6:1–2:

> Brothers and sisters, if someone is caught in a sin, you who live by the Spirit should restore that person gently. But watch yourselves, or you also may be tempted. Carry each other's burdens, and in this way you will fulfill the law of Christ.

Restore a person gently. Watch yourself. Carry each other's burdens. These are instructions of love and concern, not control or harshness.

It's important to factor in Matthew 7 here. Jesus tells us to take "logs" out of our own eyes so we can see clearly to take "specks" out of other people's eyes (vv. 3–5 NASB). In other words, we must deal with our own issues first. We aren't called to judge the specks we see in others but to help them see theirs. Unless we recognize our own issues, then our tendency is to judge people, but if we recognize we are all saved by grace, then our tone becomes gentler. We are moved by love and concern for the other person.

We have other processes in place at our church, too, so we can regularly connect and care for people. For instance, Life Group leaders are encouraged to contact all people in their group each week. We don't want anybody to fall through the cracks.

Recently I (Jim) was privileged to see God's method of discipline work again. A man who had accepted Christ a few years ago had grown in amazing ways and was involved in a Life Group. About three months ago he just disappeared from our weekend services. Immediately his team leader began to call. After a couple of weeks of no response, we contacted his Life Group leader. We learned that the man had begun to question our theology because of a radio program he was listening to and was now looking at a different church. He had come to the group with accusations and had derailed those in his group for several weeks by focusing on his new-found beliefs and trying to convince the group that they were wrong. He was asked to come with his group leader to meet with a pastor but refused. Eventually the group leader told him that he could not come to group this way. Rather than asking or searching, he had listened to an aggressive teacher who not only promoted personal preferences as doctrine but also hammered at our church. The young man finally told his home group leader that he would no longer attend.

As leaders, we began to pursue the young man, asking to sit with him and talk through his questions. He said he had no questions. We reminded him that he had many spiritual family members who had helped him come to know Jesus in our church. We had helped him move to a new house and ministered to him in many ways. I challenged him to read some books written by great pastors he had trusted in the past, trying to help him understand that the issue he was separating over was not worth the separation. We were careful not to attack the other church, because we did not think the issue was important enough to fight about. We told him people can be Christians and disagree about this issue.

But the young man made it clear that he had made up his mind. So we assured him he was loved and that we would be there in a second if he ever needed us. I began to text him at times just to let him know he was missed. Others saw him at a store or a coffee shop and hugged him and told him they missed him. After two months we got the call. He had begun to feel the difference and realized he had walked away from his spiritual family. He found that his new church attacked not just our church but most churches and for silly reasons. They did not do life together—they merely met once a week, and the messages were divisive in nature. He had been won to Jesus and become part of our family. It was in the family he had been lovingly confronted—and it was a family that he missed. It has been amazing to see the body work together to seek and restore this drifting person, and amazing to see the effect on him. God's plan truly does work.

7

While They Are Away from Home

If you have a loved one who has walked away from the
faith and has also left home, what do you do while they
are away? There is no playbook that tells you specifically
what to do in these difficult times.

When my son Christian was at his worst, living in a homeless
shelter, we longed to help him, but we knew that he needed to
hit bottom and experience what that felt like, so we resolved to
leave him there. This was very difficult for us to do as parents.

Christian was emailing Kiela, a girl he had dated earlier,
and she got him out of the shelter against our wishes. After
he understood that he could not live with us, he immediately
moved in with her, an unbeliever. Soon, he started using drugs
again. Christian was not anti-God during this time, but he
definitely was not walking with Him. We were troubled on
many levels by his actions and attitudes, but we wanted to

keep the relationship with him open and also build a relationship with his girlfriend. We wanted to show her that we loved her, even though we didn't agree with all their decisions.

They ran low on money and asked to come live with us, but we said no, this was not God's plan for a relationship and we would not support it under our roof. We wouldn't even let them sleep in the same room when they came to visit. Over time, Lori developed a friendship with Kiela, going shopping or out to lunch together. One day, Kiela said to Lori, "You know, Christian and I are not doing very well. It's just hard work being in a relationship." She added that she had no idea what it meant to have a relationship with God but was sincerely interested, although she felt her prayers bounced off the ceiling.

Lori said, "Are you asking my opinion?"

Kiela said, "Yes. You and Jim have been married for a long time."

Lori said, "You need Jesus in your life. That means that you need to surrender your life to Jesus as Lord and Savior." She shared that Jesus saves us when we place our faith in Him, and faith leads to obedience because we are grateful for His death on the cross. It also leads to trust as we realize that everything God asks us to do is because He loves us. When we trust and obey Jesus, He begins to bless as we build our lives on His directions and promises. Lori told Kiela directly, "God won't bless your relationship if you're being sexually active outside of marriage."

Kiela didn't know the Bible said anything about that. She wasn't anti-God either; she just didn't know much about Jesus, His grace, forgiveness, restoration, and love. Kiela moved out of where she and Christian were living together and moved in with us. She wanted Jesus in her life, and she wanted the relationship between her and Christian to work. Christian was mad at us because we wouldn't let them both live with us unmarried, although he still knew we loved him. One day I said, "Christian, you both need Jesus in your life. Lori and I are trying to help your relationship, not hurt it."

The great news was that Kiela gave her life to the Lord.

And more great news is that soon Christian gave his life to the Lord too, and things began to change. After Kiela received Christ, she wanted to be baptized the very next Sunday. I slipped back into town from a camping weekend with our Life Group in time for our church's third service so I could perform her baptism.

Standing beside the baptismal, I explained to the congregation that Kiela was my son's girlfriend and she had just given her life to the Lord. Next to me were Lori, my parents and family, Kiela's family, and Christian. After I baptized Kiela, I turned to the right and nodded to leaders on the platform to finish the service. But the whole room went quiet and continued to look at me. The worship pastor pointed to my left, and I turned to see my son sitting in the baptismal, looking at me expectantly. Christian had tricked me into believing that only Kiela was ready for baptism.

I didn't know what to say. Tears ran down my son's face. I was crying and Lori was a mess. My younger sons smiled broadly. Many in the congregation knew our family's prodigal story, and many were crying. Speechless and emotionally broken, I baptized my son. The church people stood to their feet and applauded.

Before long Kiela and Christian were married, and I performed the ceremony. They're in ministry together today.

Not every story will turn out like that, but it's helpful to hear that some stories do have happy endings. Maybe you're not at that place yet with your children. It's a time of full-blown tension in your home. What do you do?

Surviving the Disaster

I (Bill) have found that this is how people tend to respond in the middle of a family disaster:

- Most people go through denial, blaming others, or feeling numb.
- Some turn to alcohol or drugs, but the mess doesn't go away.
- Some give in to depression and even consider suicide.
- Some give themselves over to guilt, dwelling on "if only," tormenting themselves with how they may have prevented the disaster. They may confess personal sins over and over. (I've even made up sins I might have committed to make up for ones I can't remember.)
- Some live in constant fear because they don't know how it will end and don't feel safe.
- Some obsess with finding explanations for the rebellion.
- Some are overcome with hurt and anger to the point of rage.
- Some fall into doubt, whispering, "If God really loved me, He would come to the rescue."
- Some become bitter and hardened, believing no one understands.
- Some look for new relationships, trying to ignore the past.
- Some lose hope.

Living through the prodigal situation so deeply, I saw my need to strongly reaffirm that God is all powerful and allow my belief to turn into trust. Then I saw our need to rebuild our own marriage and family. Whenever our prodigals withdrew from us, we were a mess, as if in the wake of a hurricane. I was a bundle of contradictions. One moment I wanted the prodigals to come home, and the next moment I was afraid they would. One moment I wanted God to rebuild our family, but the next I wanted to quit. Bobbi and I determined to get right with each other, first taking our individual broken hearts to the Lord. We recommitted to each other and to be partners with God in changing our home. We pledged specific time to each other and to each of our children. We read and discussed and listened to good advice on marriage and parenting. We asked God to identify our failures and establish new directions. We called a family meeting and, in tears and repentance, asked forgiveness. We reminded ourselves, "We can't go back, but because of Jesus we can start over."

Continuing Onward

What was the father of the prodigal in Luke 15 doing while the son was away? We don't have a full understanding, but we can assume two things from the text. First, the father went about his business. He had something like a ranch or an estate, and the work of running the place continued. How do we know this? Because the older son was working in the field. Second, we know the father worked always with an eye on the road, constantly scanning the horizon, his mind on the son all the time.

This forms a picture of what the loved ones of prodigals are called to do. While our children are away, there's still work to be done. We can't succumb to the temptation to let life collapse around us. There's comfort in seeing that the prodigal's father kept on building a home in hopes that the prodigal might return. We need to minister where we are, keep going, keep functioning, keep waking up in the morning and putting on our pants one leg at a time.

At the same time, our hearts are always on our wayward child. First Thessalonians 5:16–18 exhorts us, "Always be joyful. Never stop praying. Be thankful in all circumstances, for this is God's will for you who belong to Christ Jesus" (NLT). This doesn't feel natural, but when we see that our joy can come from the Lord, and that we can be thankful *in the midst of* things—not necessarily *for* things—then this truth forms our daily guide for thinking about our prodigal. As I (Jim) asked the Lord to do whatever it would take to bring my son to his knees, to do only that and nothing more, joy followed, coming from knowing that my heavenly Father heard us, loved us, and loved our son more than we did. He was working even though we couldn't see it.

While Christian was away, I still needed to make a living, and ministry still needed to be done in other lives, so I kept working as a pastor. As a spiritual parent to others, I needed to continue to help create a spiritual home, a church, hard to leave and easy to come home to. Other prodigals were returning all around me. They were not my son, but they were other people's prodigals and God wanted their home-coming to be celebrated.

Other parents of prodigals needed encouragement and counsel, and sometimes we just got together and prayed for our wayward children. I was often tempted to be angry at my son, but I knew that would only hurt me and others. Rather than being frozen by anger or immobilized by grief,

I made the choice to move forward, to keep leading in good directions.

During this time it became very apparent that the battle was not just for our rebel son. The pain caused by Christian wasn't Lori's and mine alone. Our sons Jesse and Will were profoundly affected, and they needed to experience joy from their obedience, not just pain caused by their brother. Often we focus our energy on the absent one and forget those who are still here. Lori and I knew we could do little to stop Christian from rebelling then, but we could do a lot with our other kids. We decided to pull our boys out of school separately for a couple of weeks to go on missions trips with me. That's when I discovered the depth of their anger. Earlier they had not shared a lot because they felt that we could not take any more, so they just buried their feelings. Both had normal everyday things going on that they should have been able to discuss with us but felt they couldn't. They had anger toward us for being too strict or not strict enough with Christian. They had seen us act out anger in our marriage and this had scared them. They had questions about why God would allow this. They had looked up to their brother and he had let them down and tempted them to harmful ways. It all needed to be talked through—they needed to say honest and sometimes painful things to us. At times this caused me great guilt and I listened with a broken heart. When they stopped sharing because they could see I was hurt, I encouraged them to get it all out and that it was okay. Because of this hard and painful work done with my sons, new levels of relationship were built. With the Lord's help, I was able to come alongside them.

One event really changed Will's heart. Will and I had gone to Mexico to do missions work. As I shared earlier, Christian had been allowed out of jail to start a rehab program, was kicked out and dropped off at a homeless shelter, and demanded we come and get him. Will thought I would get us immediately back on a plane to go get Christian, but Lori and I decided not to drop everything and run to Christian this time. Yes, it was a crisis, but the time I was spending with Will was desperately needed too. So I stayed in Mexico with Will and finished the trip before even going to see Christian. This showed my son Will that he was just as loved as Christian was. It showed him that doing the right things is celebrated too.

Our middle son, Jesse, on a later trip, helped me train pastors in Israel. Teaching the story of the prodigal son together, we asked the question, who do you most relate to in that story? Jesse started by opening up himself and answered the question first by saying he was most like the older brother because he was angry at his brother Christian. He shared with the pastors our story and how it affected him. I was so proud of him for being honest, and not only did it set the tone of honesty for the other pastors, but it opened the door to feelings Jesse had not shared with me. So that's when we began to talk and pray through his feelings.

Again, this was such a difficult time, and I did not have it in me to deal with my pain, confusion, and anger in a positive way. At times I was so depressed that I was tempted to drink again for the first time in twenty-five years—and to just leave the ministry and even my family. However, as I sought the Lord (sometimes my friends grabbed me and walked me into His presence), I found strength to care for the rest of my flock. And when I went through seasons of withdrawal or bouts of anger, I was able to go back and explain and ask for forgiveness. With the help of the Holy Spirit, the Word, and your spiritual family, you can find strength even to bear spiritual fruit.

While Christian was away from home, at his most difficult times, I kept up contact through text messages and phone calls. Some he welcomed, and some he did not. I kept contacting him anyway, even if he became angry and said painful things. Sometimes I lost my temper and said wrong things also, but I kept contacting him because I didn't want our relationship—however minimal—to wither away to nothing. Often he called me a hypocrite or said he hated me or wished I was dead, but I constantly told him I loved him.

Lori and I continually talked and prayed through issues and sought all the help possible. Jesus said that a house divided cannot stand, and the devil was working to bring our home down around our ears. What all our kids needed most was for us to be a united couple. That could only happen if we abided in Christ. As we each went to the Lord individually, we'd gain ability to love and forgive each other and hope for reaching our kids somehow, sometime. We made sure our spiritual family knew we needed help, and Lori and I each had trusted spiritual family members who could hear us out and pray with us.

Bobbi and I (Bill) were challenged to help our own family with the fallout a prodigal leaves behind and learn the need for forgiveness and the power of apology. Jim left home at age nineteen after being a prodigal in our house for several years, and this had affected our daughters. One became angry with me and this in part led to her own prodigal season. She felt the tension and chaos in our house, and blamed me and Jim for causing that mess. I must have asked for her forgiveness for five years. When Jim finally came back, she had a hard time forgiving him and wanted nothing to do with him. Jim apologized over and over. He tried everything to make things right, and finally said he was done trying. He said angrily, "It's her issue and I am not going to say sorry again." He asked me, "How many times does a person have to say sorry?" I shared what the Lord had taught me, that that is the wrong question. The right question is, how many times does she need you to say it? As long as a person needs it, then say it and say it again, and keep saying it until it's no longer an issue.

God is the God of restored relationships, but the devil is the divider of people. The devil will stir up hurts and feelings of unforgiveness time and time again. Paul reminds us in Ephesians 6:10 that we don't fight against flesh and blood but against spiritual forces—the real enemy is in the spiritual realm pulling the strings. Whether we are the prodigal who has hurt others, or we have wrongly hurt someone else, we need to help those we have hurt put down the burden the devil puts on them. A person might approach us and need us to say we're sorry again. If we get defensive, then tension will escalate, but if we just go ahead and apologize again, then we cut off the devil's strategy. The apology can be part of a discussion, or as simple as saying sincerely, "You're right, I did do that. It was wrong. Please forgive me again."

In my (Bill's) life, I had to work to forgive the man who molested me at age ten. I would forgive him, but then something would trigger a memory, and I would be angry or upset or hurt all over again, so I would need to go to the Lord and forgive the man again. Even today, so many years later, memories come up and I feel hurt, and I need to say, "Lord, I've forgiven this person a thousand times. Please help me forgive once more." That's liberating.

If we are the ones who have done wrong, we must maintain a spirit of repentance. A spirit of repentance means that we change our attitude toward what we have done and toward the one we have hurt. We cannot go back and we need not beat ourselves up again and again as if God hasn't forgiven us. But we must understand that those we have hurt in the past may still be affected. When a prodigal comes home, they have much work to do in the lives of those hurt. That work of love may take the rest of their lives.

If we are ones who have been hurt, we need to maintain a spirit of forgiveness and remember that forgiveness is not a one-time decision. Depending on how deep the wound is, we may need to choose to forgive a thousand times.

There's such a tremendous ministry in apologizing and being forgiven. If I think I've done something wrong to somebody, then I try to go ask for their forgiveness without delay. I'll just say, "Hey, can we talk a minute? I think I need to ask for your forgiveness," and then I'll explain what I think happened. Sometimes I've misread the situation, and the person says, "Oh, that was no big deal." But other times, a genuine grievance has occurred. So I want to be proactive, and not let anything I've done or said divide me from others and give the devil a possible foothold in our lives.

Ten Best Practices

When you're in pain, principles are hard to apply. The sin of others complicates things, and black-and-white answers aren't easy to figure out. That said, below are some helpful practices regarding what you can do while your prodigal is away.

1. Pray. Pray. Pray. And keep praying!

Bathe each day in prayer. Pray before and after (and during) each interaction with your prodigal. Get on your knees before God. Pray constantly, without ceasing, for your prodigal. We don't understand completely how prayer works, nor does God tell us. But what He does tell us about prayer is to do it. Just do it. "Is anyone among you in trouble? Let him pray" (James 5:13).

Sometimes the answers to our prayers arrive much later. We don't understand God's timing, but we know God sometimes seems silent when He isn't silent at all. His timing is just different from ours. Ephesians 6:18 encourages us to "pray at all times in the Spirit, with all prayer and supplication."

An excellent passage for parents of prodigals is Philippians 4:6–7. It sounds trite to say "don't worry," but we can truly not worry if we are soaking ourselves in prayer, seeking the Lord's face. Trust God. Lean on God's promises. Stay in His Word. Don't let yourself be pulled away from God.

> Do not be anxious about anything, but in every situation, by prayer and petition, with thanksgiving, present your requests to God. And the peace of God, which transcends all understanding, will guard your hearts and your minds in Christ Jesus. (Phil. 4:6–7)

Be honest with God about your frustrations. He can take it. In the Psalms—David's prayer journal—he often asked, "Lord, why are You so far from me?" But he'd conclude with a statement of trust. That's what praying and Scripture can do for us—take us from a place of fear to a place of faith. We may be filled with fear that our child will end up in the worst possible place and ruin their life. Praying reminds us that even if the worst happens, God can work all things out for good for those who love Him and are called according to His purpose (Rom. 8:28). In other words, He can step in and make the worst thing into something that has eternal good.

2. Guard your marriage.

The stress of dealing with prodigal children can really rip apart a marriage. Parents feel acute tension between wanting to protect their children and letting them experience the pain of their own mistakes. Lori was terrified of Christian being in an adult jail for the first time (he had been in a juvenile jail several times). She wanted us to bail Christian out, but I said no. At that time, Christian wasn't willing to go to rehab. Later when he was released, sure enough, he immediately began partying again. Throughout these trials, we needed to guard our marriage.

It's helpful not to lay the blame on a spouse. Laying guilt trips doesn't do anybody any good. Certainly parents make mistakes, but kids ultimately make their own choices, and remember there is our part, their part, and God's part in the equation.

With Lori and me, as I have mentioned, it was essential to get on the same page. That meant we needed to frequently check in to see how the other was doing. If Christian made a request of either of us, then we needed to check with the other spouse before making a decision. Prodigal children can be great at being rude, demanding, and manipulative. Lori and I needed to create a unified front.

3. Hand your prodigal over to God.

It's hard to remember that God loves your prodigal even more than you love them, but He does. God is working, but

He's a tremendous respecter of people's choices, and we can get frustrated because we think God is taking too long or not doing enough. Then we need to lean into God and trust Him more fully than ever before.

When we disagreed about Christian going to adult jail, Lori feared that something evil would be done to him by an older adult. We had argued about it and eventually agreed (Lori reluctantly) to leave him in jail until the courts let him go. While he was in jail, one of the guys in our church's recovery program got saved. He had been dodging arrest warrants, so we counseled him to be repentant and face the consequences with God's help. He turned himself in and went to jail, but with a changed heart. He was a big dude, and he set out to speak to young men who appeared to be there for the first time. He did not know my son from Adam, but he walked right up to Christian, held out his Bible, and said, "You and I are going to do a Bible study together. Get up and come with me." Christian later told me that he got up because the man was huge and tattooed and he was afraid. Christian had not been willing to hear anything about God for several years, but he heard it from that man. No one but God knew that those two men would be in that jail at the same time. What had caused Lori the greatest fear became a big step in the right direction.

Have you come to the place where you are ready to give up? Do you wish you had never had children? Are you looking for the place where parents resign? Have you caught yourself wishing that you or your child would die so the pain could stop? I (Bill) cowered in the corner of despair as my children wandered from God. But I learned to say to myself, GIVE THEM BACK TO GOD!

Actually, the pain of having a prodigal isn't unlike so many other pains parents face. If your child is taken out of your life by miscarriage, crib death, or some other tragedy, or is snatched by another's choices, by divorce, or a court decision, what do you do? If your child rebels against God, the law, and your own authority, what do you do?

I say, "GIVE THEM BACK!"

I don't mean give up on them. Let me explain. You see, when my son was MY son, I hadn't been a good father and he hadn't been a good son, and we were a mess. But from the day he became God's son, he has been a joy to me.

You may ask, "But how can we give children back? They were never ours in the first place!" That is true. Part of the reason my marriage and family became such a mess is that I thought they were MY marriage and family. Before God could begin to heal our hearts and home, I needed to give myself and the family back to the God who created us. That is, I needed to acknowledge that we belonged to Him.

That's your invitation as well.

First, hand over to God your sorrows, agonies, stresses, and anxieties. Jesus said,

Are you tired? Worn out? Burned out on religion? Come to me. Get away with me and you'll recover your life. I'll show you how to take a real rest. Walk with me and work with me—watch how I do it. Learn the unforced rhythms of grace. I won't lay anything heavy or ill-fitting on you. Keep company with me and you'll learn to live freely and lightly. (Matt. 11:28–30 MSG)

Then hand your children over to Him. Take your hands off. GIVE THEM BACK TO GOD. He can handle them.

4. Keep the relationship open.

We counsel a lot of parents with rebellious children, and often, after trying everything they could, they swing the pendulum to the other side and want to cut all ties with their kids. They may quote Scriptures about not associating with a so-called brother who is sexually immoral (1 Cor. 5:11). But this was geared toward church discipline for someone who is pretending to be a Christian—a hypocrite. Jesus had a different approach for non-Christians. He always sought the lost and prodigals, but with pretenders, he only verbally confronted. As well, we have an added responsibility to reach out to our own children. We certainly cannot support their sin, but we must keep the door open to relationship. Our counsel is not to cut ties but always to go the other direction and maintain the relationship. This isn't easy. A lot of emotions can get in the way—anger, grief, depression, sorrow, guilt. And a lot of actions can get in the way. Sometimes there are communication blocks, social stigmas, or legal implications.

We know of parents who raised a son and daughter to walk close to the Lord, and both did so while in high school. In college, the son continued to walk with God. But the daughter got into a dating relationship with a guy who wasn't a believer. The relationship progressed and they decided to get married. The parents didn't like the idea of their daughter marrying this guy (basically an atheist), and they faced a tough decision: How could they offer their blessings on a marriage they didn't approve of? They didn't feel like going to the wedding, much less blessing it.

But after counsel and prayer, the parents decided that though they couldn't rescue their daughter from her poor choices, they would lead with love and try to keep the relationship open. So they went to the wedding, and her father walked her down the aisle. It proved difficult all around. After about a year together, the husband became abusive, and the young couple soon divorced, but at least the daughter knew she could talk to her parents. Her relationship with her parents was still intact.

You might be extremely troubled by the path your child has chosen, but keep on loving and praying. Don't turn your back on your child. Keep the relationship open.

5. Connect with people who encourage you.

Parents of a prodigal can't go it alone. There are too many things to process. Find somebody in the church who loves you with God's grace and can come alongside you, who can cry with you in the night and pray with you in need. Learn to humbly accept help from your church family.

When there's trouble in a family, sometimes the parents' first thought is to flee. They want to separate themselves from family and friends, because they feel embarrassed or guilty. It's true: sometimes people in the church (or outside) will heap accusations on the parents of a prodigal. They will say that you weren't a good parent. They will gossip or offer unsolicited advice that only makes you feel the sting of shame. The best counsel is just to let this blow right past you, forgive people of their insensitivity, and don't hold grudges. But work to connect with people who encourage you. Don't go through this season in isolation.

6. Keep functioning.

This seems straightforward, but you may struggle with this because when a prodigal is in your life, you're in crisis mode. Adrenaline is flowing. Your body is in a state of tension. The biggest task at hand seems to be getting through the crisis.

But that same crisis may take a lot of time to resolve—maybe years, decades. It's very difficult to operate in crisis mode long term, so part of the solution is to keep functioning. Practice self-care. Eat right. Exercise. Get lots of sleep. Go for walks where it's just you and God.

Remember that you have a life apart from your prodigal. You have a spouse. You have friends. You have other children. You have a job, hobbies, a ministry.

So keep going. Keep living. Keep doing the work around you.

7. Don't succumb to sin yourself.

When life hands you chaos, it's tempting to turn to something harmful to alleviate the pain. Fathers of prodigals may start drinking or turn to porn. Mothers may turn to overspending or overeating or bitterness. None of these will help. The only place to turn is to the Lord.

At age forty-one, my (Bill's) job at the church was busy, but it felt like the ministry was failing. My marriage was difficult, bills overwhelming, children out of control. One day, a married woman, a church member, entered my office and told me directly that she wanted to have an affair with me.

Her words were so shocking. So blatant. I remembered a seminary professor saying, "I don't care how ugly you are, if you are looking to be immoral, the devil will always provide an opportunity."

My ego surged at the flattering offer. I nearly lost control, and my mind wondered, *Maybe this could all work out okay. My life's a mess anyway. This surely couldn't hurt.*

By God's grace, I didn't succumb to temptation but took out a piece of paper, and with her seeing what I was doing, I drew a line down the middle of the paper. On one side I wrote the positives of the affair and on the other side the negatives and what it would cost. Sin might be pleasurable for a moment, but the list of cons was huge. Having an affair wasn't going to improve anything, and would ruin so much. I'd lose my best friend—my wife Bobbi. My children would be hurt for life. If I tried to keep the affair a secret, it would rip me apart. Most of all, I would be sinning against my Savior.

Right away I told my wife about it. Bless her heart, Bobbi went to the woman and ministered to her, counseled, and prayed with her. Here's the amazing twist: Over time, we moved away, but ten years later I ran into the woman at an airport. She said, "Bill, you were the first man who didn't use me. Since then, I've come back to the Lord. And not only me, but my husband, children, and mother have all come to the Lord."

8. *Never stop loving your prodigal.*

First Corinthians 14:1 says, "Follow the way of love." This instruction comes after an entire chapter that's dedicated to love. The gist of chapter 13 is that we can have much in our lives, but without love, none of it is worth anything. In dealing with your prodigal, you may need to read 1 Corinthians 13 again and again. Memorize the passage. Are we constantly loving our prodigal? Are we patient with our prodigal? Are we kind to our prodigal? Are we easily angered with our prodigal? Are we dishonoring or slandering our prodigal? Are we keeping a record of our prodigal's wrongs? Even while setting boundaries, are we protecting our prodigal, trusting him to God, hoping for him, and persevering with him?

These are the ways of love.

9. Don't be afraid to let your prodigal experience pain.

This principle might sound strange, but parents can be tempted to jump in and "fix" the prodigal's problems. Sometimes the most loving thing we can do is let our prodigal feel the effects of their sin.

Is it always necessary to let your prodigal feel the full brunt of their sin? The biblical answer seems to be no. God, in His grace, doesn't always allow us to feel the full consequences of sin. So definitely we need wisdom and may make some mistakes. You might think you are letting your prodigal hit rock bottom only to find there is another "bottom" below that.

Bobbi and I (Bill) exhausted ourselves and our resources and our family and friends while Jim kept digging his hole deeper and deeper. Bobbi began to pray, "Lord, please do whatever it takes for our children to come to you." We had done everything in our power to rescue Jim, but it wasn't working. We needed to let God do His work.

What exactly is rock bottom? It's different for different prodigals. For my daughter, it took her pregnancy to turn her around. For Jim, it was after he had lost control of his drinking and faced losing his wrestling career. There was nowhere to turn but to the Lord.

I (Jim) mentioned how when Christian was in jail, the guy from our recovery ministry did a Bible study with him. The amazing thing is that Christian would not have experienced that Bible study if we had rescued him and bailed him out of jail.

10. *Remember that Jesus never leaves you.*

The parent of a prodigal may feel alone, but there's great comfort in Hebrews 13:5, where God says, "Never will I leave you; never will I forsake you." Be encouraged by Isaiah 41:10: "So do not fear, for I am with you; do not be dismayed, for I am your God. I will strengthen you and help you; I will uphold you with my righteous right hand."

A woman experienced much pain due to her children's sinful ways. Later, her children came back to the Lord, and she was asked how she got through that difficult time. She described how she literally wrote out encouraging Bible verses on big sheets of paper and placed them all around her house. Everywhere she looked she saw God's encouragement. Remember that Jesus never leaves you alone.

Hope for Today

The difficult years aren't forgotten, but in all our families—Bill, Jim, and Christian—we have worked hard to replace painful memories with positive ones. Christian and Kiela are an integral part of our family today, and their little Kaden is such a blessing. Jim is restored to Bill and Bobbi, and so are all their daughters.

It can be tempting to burn bridges in a relationship. Things get so strained that you want to leave. But hang in there. Bright futures do arrive. Sometimes we won't see them until much later, but God is a God of hope. Keep praying, keep trusting God, keep working and ministering and living.

God is always at work in the lives of the people we love.

8

While They Are Away from Church

In the story of the prodigal son, think of the older son as a picture of the church and imagine a completely different scenario that might have played out in his life . . .

There once was a good father who had two sons. The younger said to his father, "Dad, give me my share of the estate now instead of when you die."

So the good father chose to respect his son's free choice, even though his son was heading in the wrong direction, and he gave the younger son what he asked for.

The boy left town and set out for a distant country. There, he squandered his wealth in wild living. After everything was gone, a severe famine came upon the land. People everywhere were in need. The younger son was broke and hungry and couldn't get a job that paid a living wage. So he took work at the only place he could find—a pig farm. Even then, the young man's wages were low, and he often grew so hungry that he eyed the pigs with jealousy. The pigs ate slop, but at least they were eating.

Now here's where we need some imagination. What if *meanwhile back at the ranch . . .*

The older brother stayed home, did his job, ministered to other people, stayed out of trouble, did what his father asked of him. The older brother understood his role in the family—it was to help his good father. He knew the younger brother's wild living put tremendous strain on the family, so the older brother prayed *for* his dad, and he prayed *with* his dad. He prayed that his little brother would come to his senses, repent, and return home. He also prayed for his little brother's safety, even in the midst of the boy's rebellion. He prayed that God would allow the boy to hit bottom but be redeemed and restored through the process.

Regularly, the older brother worked to keep in contact with the younger brother. The older brother wrote him letters, phoned him, texted him, and wrote on his Facebook page. He talked to the boy in whatever capacity the boy allowed, and sometimes that changed, depending on the younger brother's moods. Sometimes the younger brother was receptive to the older brother's calls and letters. At other times, the younger brother was angry, cold, and distant. He acted like he wanted nothing to do with his big brother. But the older brother knew his little brother had been deceived and was speaking out of emptiness, so he didn't let the younger brother's immaturity get him down. He took the high road. He kept being the forgiving person. He kept reaching out. He cared too much *not* to intrude.

The older brother's messages to his younger brother were warm, relaxed, and welcoming, not condemning, even though he abhorred the younger brother's actions. He always sought to make sure his little brother knew their dad loved and missed him. When the younger brother would go on a tirade about how their father had failed, the older brother always listened and tried to be a peacemaker, sharing that their father's intentions were always for his good.

In the meantime, life wasn't always easy as the older brother. He grieved for his sibling. He missed him. He lamented that their once-happy family now felt severed and bruised. There was more work to do around the farm with the younger brother away, and often the older brother needed to shoulder extra responsibilities. He was sincerely upset with his younger brother's actions, and he worked to find the balance between expressing raw truth and expressing that truth in love.

The older brother continually challenged himself by reading 1 Corinthians 13 and applying its directives to how he acted and felt toward his younger brother. The older brother invited the fullness of the Holy Spirit into his life and asked for God's help in being patient and kind to his younger brother. He didn't want to dishonor his brother, even though his brother had dishonored the family. He didn't want to keep any record of wrongs, even though the brother had done much that could be recorded. The older brother continually hoped for the younger brother's return. He prayed that God would help him persevere while they waited.

The older brother filled his mind and heart with other passages of Scripture about how he should respond in his pain. He reminded himself that we are to "encourage one another" (1 Thess. 5:11), and "carry each other's burdens"

(Gal. 6:2), and "forgive one another" (Eph. 4:2), and "serve one another humbly in love" (Gal. 5:13).

When friends of the family wondered where the younger brother was, the older brother refused to gossip and so dishonor his little brother. He refused to join anyone in slandering his brother. He refused to grumble against him (James 5:9).

When the older brother became discouraged (and there were definitely days when this happened), he reminded himself that we "groan" because we long to be clothed with our heavenly dwelling (2 Cor. 5:2). But someday the world would be made right, so there was hope. He deliberately chose not to be anxious about anything, but to cast all cares and concerns upon God (Phil. 4:6) and to set his mind on things above, not on earthly things (Col. 3:2). He rejoiced in God and in God's strength. He focused on the goodness and graciousness of God.

At the end of every day, when that day's work was done, the older brother walked with his good father to the end of the driveway. They each took a good long look toward the end of the road, as far as either man could look. They searched the horizon, always hoping that they could see the younger brother returning home.

Time passed.

The great day finally came. The younger brother came to his senses, realized even his father's servants had food to spare, and headed home.

While he was a long way off, both his father and older brother saw him and were filled with compassion for him. They ran to the younger brother, threw their arms around him, and welcomed him home.

The son said, "Father, I've sinned against heaven and this family. I'm no longer worthy to be called your son. And, brother, I've sinned against you too. Will you please for-give me?"The father and older brother said to the servants, "Quick, let's have a feast and celebrate. For our family mem-ber who was once lost is now found!"

And together they all began to celebrate!

Lives in Relationship

When Jesus told this story, He was revealing the heart He would have liked the Pharisees to have toward the lost sheep of Israel. Often Jesus heard the criticism from the Jews that He would eat with sinners. In response, Jesus on one occa-sion had made it clear that He had not come for the well but the sick. In our time, we as God's people represent the older brother. Can you see how your church might be much like the older son in the biblical version? Or is your church more like the imagined story I just shared? That's our prayer for churches today—that we'd look at the story of the prodigal son, ask ourselves what the older brother should have done, and then live that way, because there are prodigals all around us in our churches and circling outside.

Remember the definition of a prodigal—a person who once got saved (or appeared to have been saved) but then drifted away from the Lord and no longer claims to follow Jesus. Some prodigals have left the church. Some have stayed. So, as a church, what do we do with prodigals?

First—and it sounds overly obvious—we should notice that people are away from church (the spiritual family). Be aware. We can't care for prodigals if we don't know who the prodigals are. Our care begins through intentionality and relationships. We must also have relational systems in place that allow us to know how other people are doing spiritually.

The best place to do this is through groups of people living in community. You can call them Life Groups like we do at Real Life Ministries or something else, but bottom line, these are people in a church who gather together regularly for the purpose of discipleship within relationship.

Why do this? So people are known within a body of believers. Too often we think that spiritual maturity comes about by simply knowing more about God. Certainly it's good for all believers to know and study Scripture, but true spiritual maturity happens when we treat each other with love. So we encourage all Christians to get involved in groups that enable community.

The Bible instructs us to confess our sin to one another (James 5:16). We take this commandment seriously and literally at Real Life Ministries, and we encourage people to do this in the context of the relationships formed in their small groups. Certainly there are boundaries surrounding this. Men are instructed to confess to other men, and women to other women. The reason for confessing is so each person would experience repentance and restoration within a body of believers. Restoration is always the goal. We want to walk the road together as a church, and we recognize that all people sin, including people who love Jesus, so nobody is judging or condemning anybody else.

Confession can take many forms. We "confess" any time we tell trusted people the truth about what's happening in our lives. We "confess" when we say things like "I feel far away from the Lord right now," or "I'm really struggling in this area of my life," or "I just don't understand why God allows this particular thing to happen," or "Please pray for me in this area." The emphasis isn't so much that we explain in detail all the sordid specifics about our sin, but that we are honest with one another. We don't keep secrets from one another. We recognize that lives are best lived in transparency and vulnerability. When this happens, we can talk about what truly matters. We can become mature believers together, believers who truly follow Jesus, allow Jesus to transform our lives, and join with Jesus in the incredible mission of making other disciples.

Here's our point. We need to establish systems in our churches that allow for these kinds of honest relationships to happen. If there's no relationship, then it is much more difficult to know who is prodigal and to what degree. Sure, overt sins such as affairs are usually made known. But what if people knew each other well enough and were honest enough that it never got to the point of the affair? What if transparency and honesty led to sharing the temptation before it became an action? So often the church doesn't know what is really happening until it's big and dramatic. At that point, many either sweep it under the carpet or attack the sinner with little mercy in the name of Scripture. This is reactionary rather than preventative. So much could be avoided if we understood true spiritual maturity and discipled people toward it in our churches. In relationship, we can provide real strength to withstand temptation; and it's in real relationship that we notice the prodigal and begin to function rightly to do our part to provide the best opportunity to bring them home.

In the biblical story of the prodigal son (not the version as we've told it at the start of this chapter), remember that when the younger brother came home and the household started to celebrate, the older brother was alone out in the fields. Why wasn't he invited to the party? Or if he was invited, then why didn't he initially go? And why was he out in the fields alone? Where were the workers helping him?

It could be a case of a man who was separated from relationships. He'd already let bitterness and anger flare up in his life. He had isolated himself from others. Or maybe he had become critical and mean-spirited and unforgiving so no one wanted to be around him. Undoubtedly, we have too many "older brothers" in the church today, people who are isolated from others, bitter, and who make it hard for the younger brothers to come home.

Real relationships are the means to grow together as disciples of Jesus. We must have relationships, because Jesus's invitation to all of us is to become spiritually mature together.

Ten Helpful Practices for Churches

Beyond creating the system to identify who the prodigals are in our churches, how do we best care for prodigals? Following are ten helpful practices:

1. Understand it's our job to look for strays.

What is the job of a church and, subsequently, our job as people who make up the church? Actually, it's the Lord's command that we search for strays. Often we think only of the so-called main functions of a church. But when we see all the functions of a church taken together, we see that it is most definitely our job as Christians to minister to people—including prodigals.

According to Acts 2:42, the main functions of a New Testament church are to devote ourselves to teaching, fellowship, the breaking of bread (the Lord's Supper), and prayer. Acts 1:8 describes a church that's a witness in progressively larger spheres of influence—the immediate city, the region, and the ends of the earth. Ephesians 4:12–16 describes believers who are equipped for the work of ministry, building up the body of Christ until we all attain spiritual maturity.

Perhaps Ezekiel 34 is a passage that most directly pertains to prodigals. The passage describes ministers who "search for the lost and bring back the strays." This passage works in tandem with several New Testament passages we've described in this book, such as the parables of the lost sheep (Luke 15:1–7), the lost coin (Luke 15:8–10), and the prodigal son (Luke 15:11–32).

The bottom line is that this is the work we are called to do. If we don't care about prodigals, then we're not doing the work God has called us to do.

One of the practical components of this is just careful logistics and record keeping. Where are your people and where are they spiritually? Church leadership needs to know

- who is responsible for seeking the prodigals
- who has committed to being disciple makers
- how they are going to know those assigned to them
- how they are going to track the involvement of those assigned to them
- how the church can identify those who are infant disciples, child disciples, young adults, or reproducing spiritual adult disciples

Here are some descriptions that I (Bill) devised to help identify people and discover needs the church may meet:

A spiritual infant needs nurture and protection. The spiritual adults can mobilize the church to care for infant Christians like a mother cares for a baby.

A spiritual child needs nurture, protection, and also teaching. The spiritual adults can oversee meeting these needs.

A spiritually young adult disciple needs teaching, discipline, and apprenticeship. Spiritual adults take on these apprentices in caring for baby and child Christians the same way a good father cares for his children.

A spiritual parent disciple who is in the process of making disciples needs support, and other spiritually adult parents need to support them and release them to reproduce.

A missing, sick, or straying disciple needs to be sought and restored. The spiritual adults can identify the needs and oversee the confronting and disciplining of prodigals.

Professing Christians who are in rebellion against God and are clearly prodigals need the spiritual adults to go in search of them.

The unsaved need someone to lead them to Jesus. The spiritual adults can model, oversee, and implement the Great Commission.

This is not about putting labels on people but about knowing them and caring for them in the best ways.

2. Undertake the ministry of prayer for prodigals.

Prayer is possibly the greatest thing any believer can do in the care of prodigals. We should never dismiss prayer as the "only" thing we can do or as the last resort. We can keep an ongoing list of needy people and simply pray for those people regularly.

What do our prayers look like? Pray that a rich environment would be created in the church beforehand so fewer prodigals would leave, pray for prodigals while they are gone, pray for prodigals to return home safely, and pray for prodigals who are making the transition back into a life of fellowship. Pray for our church to strengthen the support systems to receive back a prodigal.

Join with other parents and spouses who have prodigals. One of the greatest things we can say to people is "I'm praying for you," and then actually pray.

3. Continue to reach out to prodigals.

If we have a relationship already established with a person who becomes a prodigal, then we must seek to keep that relationship going. It is often easier for people who aren't related to a prodigal to speak truth into that person's life. When it comes to receiving advice, kids often listen better to people other than their parents. Husbands and wives often listen to others better than they listen to their spouses.

When my son Christian was in rehab, he needed a bicycle to get around town. A man who'd known Christian from church went out and got him a bike. This man was at a place where he could care for Christian more easily than I could, and I loved the man for doing that.

4. Just break the ice with prodigals.

If a prodigal has left, sometimes the initial contact is the hardest part of connecting with a person. The ice will need to be broken. When this happens, I (Bill) often just send a text saying something like "I missed seeing you in church. I want you to know that I'm here for you and Jesus loves you." Or maybe it's a post on a social media page. Sometimes I'll just say something like "I don't know why, but the Lord has put you on my heart and I'm thinking of you." That gets the conversation started.

Of course, men should be careful to reach out to men, and women to women. I sometimes do contact women, but only with accountability and only if my wife knows about it. And I'll say things like "My wife and I miss you. The home group misses you."

5. Be as real and as loving as you can be with prodigals.

If you have a real relationship with a person, then there is no formula for how you speak to them. You're simply open and honest. You love the person for who they are. You have the heart to pursue this person, to chase this stray, and to help love this person back into a relationship with Jesus.

Again, that doesn't mean you condone the prodigal's actions or attitudes of the heart, but you understand that sometimes complex situations are at play, and you seek to listen to this person as much as (and more than) you talk to them.

When situations allow, you won't be afraid of confronting a person, always in hope of restoring them to Jesus. Proverbs 27:6 says, "Wounds from a friend can be trusted." You understand your role in that. You are never there to condemn or judge. But you are there to help gently restore a person to Christ. Sometimes this will mean confronting the sin in a person's life. You care too much for that person to see them continue in sinful ways.

In regard to judgment, I (Bill) have noted that while a prodigal is away from the church, it's all too easy to

- choose to self-judge. You may feel that you must take all the blame (as a pastor, leader, friend, church family). If that happens you tend to concentrate on the failures, be overwhelmed by guilt, or run after rebels, begging and making compromises with truth to bring them back.

- choose to judge the rebel. If that happens, you concentrate on the rebel's failures, concluding it's all their
  fault. You may withdraw and become angry, critical,
  or defensive.

- choose to look not at opportunities or potential but
  only at the sins of yourself and others. If that happens,
  you may become unforgiving or slide into hopelessness.

Better than any of these choices is a decision to go to the
Lord and His church to get help. Then you are prepared to
help the prodigal when the opportunity comes.

6. *Understand it can take time for a prodigal to trust you.*

Trust is a two-way street. Most likely, the prodigal has
broken some sort of trust relationship to be in the position
they are now in, so trust will need to be reestablished in their
relationships with others.

Yet it might also be necessary for you to establish or reestablish trust with the prodigal. Maybe you knew this person
in a different capacity than you do now. Maybe this person
thinks of themselves as a different sort of person than when
they were walking with the Lord. The person might think
you are only in their life because you want to preach at them,
so they will be wary of you now. Genuine friendship might
need to be reestablished.

You must earn the right to ask tough questions. And that
can take time.

7. *Let the Holy Spirit work in the life of the prodigal.*

Remember the three-way distinction we drew in an earlier
chapter—in the work of caring for prodigals, there is my part,

their part, and the Holy Spirit's part. John 16:8 describes how one job of the Holy Spirit is to convict people about the difference between sin and righteousness.

Meaning, it's not our job to go around trying to convict people of their sin. We see faulty examples of this all the time. Well-meaning people stand on street corners with signs telling people to repent. Friends have finger-pointing conversations with prodigal friends, pleading with a person to return to Christ.

Yet it's the Holy Spirit's job to convict. Ephesians 2:1 notes how when Christ isn't working in our hearts, when we are following the ways of this world, when we are disobeying the law of God, we are "dead" in our transgressions and sins. By contrast, God makes us "alive" in Christ (Eph. 2:5). The Holy Spirit does this regenerative work in people.

Yes, our call is to love. Yes, sometimes our job as friends is to show people the error of their ways. But it is always the Holy Spirit who ultimately does the work of conviction. Let's let God be God. If the Holy Spirit is working in a person's life, then that person is already aware of their sin. They are already alienated from God.

8. Be willing as a church to disregard appearances.

When people rebel against Jesus, the rebellion can sometimes exhibit itself in outward appearances. This is particularly true of teen culture. So, in the process of making disciples of prodigals, of rescuing the lost and bringing back strays, we may see these people coming into church dressed differently than what might be called "normal church attire." There's one simple directive here—

Welcome them anyway!

Strange hair. Strange clothes. Piercings. Tattoos. These things change and shift with culture, and what was considered countercultural twenty years ago is probably mainstream today. But here's the simple principle: if you know something shocks you, then decide not to let it shock you. Always welcome the person. Be able as a church to look past someone's appearance to their heart.

James 2 is clear that we are to welcome anyone into our churches, no matter if the person is finely dressed or wearing filthy old clothes. We aren't to show favoritism to people based on their appearance. People need to meet the good Father, no matter what they're wearing.

We are in the reclamation business in church. It doesn't matter who walks through the front doors. All people are welcome in church. We must communicate to people that they are wanted there. We will love them. Period.

9. If they return, be okay with giving assignments to prodigals.

If a person has been gone from a church and then returns, and if that person once held a position of leadership, then sometimes that person will ask to get involved in leadership again right away. When this happens, it's perfectly fine to give the prodigal an assignment, a preliminary task. Don't think of this as a hoop to jump through. Think of this as a necessary means of reestablishing trust.

For instance, in my (Bill's) work with strays, I will sometimes give a person a book to read. If the person actually reads the book, then that lets me know how serious this person is.

Depending on the failure, it may take years for them to reestablish the right to lead or serve in a visible way. Remind

189

them that it takes time to earn the right back, but in God's eyes they are forgiven. You may need to give them far less visible roles so that they can earn trust and show their humility by doing them.

10. Remember that miracles do happen.

God is in the business of changing people's lives and hearts. It's never too late for God to do a work, and a person is never too far away from the Lord to come back.

In one instance, a man's wife was unfaithful and left him. He was devastated and began to drink. The alcohol abuse was only the symptom of the desperation he felt. Regularly he'd call us—and we'd call him. We weren't willing to let him get away from the Lord. We wanted to love him through this difficult time. We'd call him, and he might be bombed. He might be standing in a liquor store. He might be hungover. We kept loving him.

And the Lord healed him. The man got right with the Lord and began to rebuild his life. Today he's a professor at a Bible college. Truly, miracles do happen.

An Attitude Shift

There's a paradigm shift that needs to happen in churches today—and it's a biblical one. We must go from being churches that are skeptical or uncaring about prodigals to churches that seek out, find, care for, and bring back strays. What's required is, first, an attitude shift and then, second, a shift in how we conduct ourselves in caring for people.

Let me (Bill) illustrate: If a Christian leader is trapped in a sinful use of the internet, what should you do? Should you relieve him of his position? Should you call him before the congregation and have him name his sin? Should you shun his whole family for what he has done? What should you do?

Not long ago I received a call from another church to help the elders as they dealt with a situation that could have destroyed lives, damaged God's reputation in the community, and stopped the forward progress of this church. The church's youth pastor confessed to a repeated immoral use of the internet. It was discovered by church volunteers, so it was becoming public within the church. Complicating matters, the youth pastor was the son of the senior pastor. The elders first met during the week with the youth pastor to address the matter among themselves.

- I arrived early and watched the key leaders greet each other, and as the critical issue was presented to them, I watched as this crisis united them instead of divided them.

- As the brother who'd failed entered the room, I watched the elders get up and embrace him and greet him as a brother and not as an enemy. I watched them gently allow the fallen brother to confess his failure and express his repentance for what he had done.

- I watched them reach out to the man with love and then ask him to step out of the room for a time while they discussed what the Lord would want them to do as leaders of the church.

- As the youth pastor left the room, I believe he was convinced the leaders loved him and would seek first what the Lord wanted and would decide what would best bring glory to Him and healing to all concerned.

The next Sunday morning I sat with the senior pastor and watched the church at worship. Even though the staff member who'd failed was his own son, I witnessed the pastor preach with great power and then heard him introduce the spokesmen for the elders, and he stood and shared the following.

The designated leader said, *"I would like to ask the pastor and elders to come and stand with me."*

I saw the elders come to stand with the pastor in united support. One of the elders had to take time off work without pay to participate.

Quietly and humbly, the elder spokesman read the following (I asked him for a copy):

God's plan for us all as sinners was and is a progression of CONFESSION, REPENTANCE, FORGIVENESS, REDEMPTION, and RESTORATION.

It is these last two, REDEMPTION and RESTORATION, that I wish to address today. I would like to ask _____ (the repentant) and _____ (wife) to come forward.

Sitting as a guest, I saw the young youth minister and his wife walk forward and stand beside the elder to be surrounded by the pastor and other elders.

The elder quietly began to speak again and said:

Two weeks ago our brother _____ came to us with a public confession. He has repented, and he has asked for and received our forgiveness. But forgiveness does not imply a lack of consequence, for there will always be consequences for our sins, even though we have been forgiven. Usually, those consequences result in a loss of blessings as a result of our separation from God.

But I wish to concentrate here and now on the two remaining parts of this process, the REDEMPTION and RESTORATION parts.

I am referring to Galatians 6:1–2, "Brethren, even if a man is caught in any trespass, you who are spiritual, restore such a one in a spirit of gentleness; each one looking to yourself lest you too be tempted. Bear one another's burdens and thus fulfill the law of Christ."

By definition, REDEMPTION is the act of purchasing back something previously sold. In this case, "trust."

By definition, RESTORATION is the act of restoring something or someone to a satisfactory state, an act of getting something back again.

The elders, in unity, and in love have set into motion our plan for _____ that we feel is biblical and consistent with God's plan.

REDEMPTION:

We have accepted _____'s resignation as Youth Minister. We know that he has enrolled and has been accepted in a program from which he will receive "treatment" and counseling.

We believe he can earn the right to have his "blemish" removed from his record. Completion of the program results in a clean slate.

RESTORATION:

It is our sincere hope to reinstate _____, or provide him with a letter of recommendation upon his successful completion of that program.

A PLAN OF CONFESSION, REPENTANCE, FORGIVENESS, REDEMPTION, AND RESTORATION:

I am asking each one of you to recognize and accept your responsibility to encourage your brother _____, to become an active member in our church's plan of redemption and restoration.

Please join the elders of your church in loving, supporting, and praying for _____ and his wife _____.

He then turned to one of the elders and asked him to pray. Following his prayer, he said, "_____[the youth minister] would like to share with you."

The elder stepped back, and the young man stepped to the pulpit and looked into the faces of the church and thanked the elders for their concern for him and his family. He stated that he was asking for the whole church's prayers and support and that he was committed to the process the elders had established. He asked the whole church to support their right decision. He went on to ask the congregation for their forgiveness and prayers, and he and his wife walked back to take their seats.

I felt honored to be a part of the process! Yes, there is a place for church discipline, but discipline always needs to be conducted according to Matthew 18, as we've discussed elsewhere in this book. And the purpose of church discipline is always to love and care for a person, to restore that person back to fellowship with Christ. Church discipline is never meant to shame a person or harm their family. If a person is already headed in a harmful direction, then the purpose of discipline is to keep them from harming themselves further.

Lessons from a Runaway Slave

The book of Philemon describes the paradigm shift we need as churches. It's a short book—you can read it straight through quite quickly. It's written in the form of a letter, and the story in the letter refers to a slave named Onesimus who has run away from his master, a prosperous Christian businessman named Philemon.

In the modern world, it seems horrible that a Christian would ever own a slave (and it is). But keep in mind that at the time of the letter's writing, there were about 120 million people in the Roman Empire, and about half—60 million— were slaves. Regardless of its moral implications, slavery was an accepted way of life back then, and Christians were involved. The Bible doesn't always confront these social ills head-on, but it sows the seeds of redemption so people will correct the wrongs from the heart.

Onesimus was a household slave. He was slightly better off than the slaves used for hard labor, such as those who worked in the galleys. But he still represented the lowest of the low. In that culture, he was property to be bought and sold. If a master didn't like a slave, then the master could beat him or even execute him—no questions asked.

The implied story is that Philemon was a good master, but slavery was still slavery, and Onesimus decided he'd had enough and ran away. He got to Rome and met the apostle Paul, who was an elderly man at this time and under house arrest (which meant he had some freedom but couldn't leave town). Onesimus helped Paul in some way, and in the process, Onesimus became a follower of Jesus.

Now, in writing the letter, Paul is sending Onesimus back to Philemon, an action that the law of the times required. A runaway slave meant lost money for the slave's owner. A runaway slave was the same as a thief. So Onesimus is guilty—no questions asked. Yet Paul appeals for clemency from Philemon, making the case that Onesimus is now a dear brother in the Lord.

"Perhaps the reason he was separated from you for a little while was that you might have him back forever—no longer as a slave, but better than a slave, as a dear brother," Paul writes. "He is very dear to me but even dearer to you, both as a fellow man as a brother in the Lord. . . . Welcome him as you would welcome me" (Philem. 15–17).

The ending of the letter implies that Philemon has a decision to make. Philemon can choose to be harsh to his runaway slave; he can play by the rules and give Onesimus the full brunt of the law. Or Philemon can choose to extend grace to his runaway. We never do find out the rest of the story. The book ends as if asking a question: What would you do if you were Philemon?

The story causes us today to ask if we are extending mercy to people. Sure, a runaway slave isn't in the exact position as a person who runs away from the Lord, but we can see tremendous parallels. People do their own thing, then come to Jesus and need to set things right with other people they've wronged. We in the church are put in the place of Philemon. Will we respond to these returned runaways with scorn and derision, or will we welcome them with open arms, as we would welcome a dear brother?

Stories of Mercy

We see good examples of how churches help prodigals—and we want to hold up those examples as stories of mercy.

In one, a girl became pregnant out of wedlock. She told her mother first. Both the daughter and the mother were very concerned—not only for the pregnancy but out of fear of the father's reaction. He was known to lose his temper.

But love got hold of this father's heart, because when he came home and heard that his daughter was pregnant, he sat for a while by himself, just thinking and praying. Then he asked his daughter to come with him. They walked outside onto the front porch where they could see a mountain far in the distance.

"Honey," he said to his daughter. "If you and I were to climb this mountain, it would be a big job. But we would do it together. The way we'd do it is to take one step at a time. That's the way this pregnancy is going to be. It's no small matter. But I want you to know I'm going to climb this mountain with you, one step at a time."

This is what our churches must become like today. Places where we climb the mountain of restoration with prodigals, where we extend love, forgiveness, care, and concern. Together, we become communities of believers that help people find their way back to God.

PART 3

THE NEW DEAL

9

When the Prodigal Returns Home

The title of this chapter immediately raises at least three questions:

1. Has the prodigal actually returned home?

Some prodigals won't return to their physical family home, some can't because they've broken the law and are in prison, some can't because they have died— murder, suicide, or accident. Some are not allowed to come home because of broken trust. Some can't come home because there is no home to come home to. Each situation calls for different responses.

2. If a prodigal returns home, have they also returned to the Lord?

It's important to discern whether your prodigal truly knows they have sinned against heaven and the Father and whether they are truly repentant. If a person has not come home to God, then returning to the physical home will only raise your hopes in vain. Your prodigal will likely leave again if they have not come to the Lord.

3. **Is the return because they have "no place else to go," or is it motivated by heart change?**

It's possible to mimic the Christian lifestyle, accumulate Bible facts, and attend a place of worship without letting any of it transform the life. Still, being around Christians and watching them can have a positive effect.

For example, I (Jim) had a recent conversation with a man who had started coming to our church. He felt that the church was the last hope for him and his family. Their lives were a wreck, and they'd reached the point of despair. He said, "We reached the end. We had $1.37, no work, and we had to get out of our rented house in two weeks. We'd tried everything and nothing worked. I was on my way to look at one more house to rent and I pulled over to the side of the road and said, 'Lord, I can't go on. If You don't show up, we are finished.'"

Testimonies of others about God's goodness and answered prayer had made him feel like a little boy looking in the window of a toy store. "I see it. I want it. But I don't have any money to get it." But just a few hours after his prayer, a man who owed him money called and said, "I want to pay you what I owe you." The house he checked on was no longer available, but on the way home he saw a brand-new "For Rent" sign. A Christian owned the house and agreed to rent it to him. In that same time frame, the man received two calls offering work and now has more work than he can do.

Seeing or hearing what God is doing for others gives a person hope. But *when God shows up* in a person's own life, it all becomes personal, and they are drawn to ask the Lord to change their own heart. This man had experienced that truth in regard to material needs, which led him to experience it on a spiritual level. We may observe what God is doing in forgiving and changing others, but the miracle of salvation and transformation needs to happen to each of us personally.

Real Homecoming

When Christian finally arrived at the place where he was ready to turn to Jesus and allow the Holy Spirit to make changes in his life, it was a great day. Christian and I (Jim) were talking about it, and I wondered aloud why it had taken him so long to "come to his senses."

He said, "Dad—it's because you never allowed me to die."

I was confused, but Christian explained what he meant. When he was a boy, I'd taken him deer hunting. We both remembered the first time he ever shot a deer. The first shot was fatal, but it didn't bring the deer down right away. Often a deer will run a short way and lie down to die. But if you chase it, adrenaline can cause a deer to run a long way and there's high potential to lose the deer. As with many first-time hunters, Christian wanted to run after the deer. But the deer needed space and time to go and die.

Christian was telling me that rather than letting him experience the full effect of his sin, I had chased him and he ran. I kept chasing him, not allowing him to hit rock bottom. My interference only caused Christian to run farther.

In the prodigal son story, the good father allowed the son to "die" all the way—that is, he allowed the son to hit rock bottom. Looking back at my own life, I see that God kept me alive physically because He knew that someday I would return. I love that He kept me alive not because of what I deserved but because He foreknew that I would eventually surrender and come home. I prayed that He would do the same for Christian. I prayed that the Lord would do nothing more or less than He needed to, to bring my son home. Even when my human father could not see where I was, God saw and kept working. Even when my son was completely outside my control, my heavenly Father knew exactly where he was and that gave me hope.

Eventually Christian hit that spot in his own life. God orchestrated the path that would bring him to the bottom, and then He was at the bottom with him. Finally, Christian was ready to come home, but that only began the process of change. In the movies we hear the phrase "They lived happily ever after," but in real life it takes time, hard work, and even pain to bring about life change. My son needed to learn and relearn so much, and it was my job (and others') to help him rebuild what had been destroyed if he would let us. As we helped him work through consequences of sin, sometimes we could only give wise counsel, and other times we helped carry some of his load. The work really begins for the parent when the child comes home. It's easy to be exhausted by their prodigal time, and to think that now they're home the battle is over, but that is not true. The difference is that now the restored prodigal is working with you rather than almost always against you.

Never forget that without real repentance, the return home is only superficial. Parents often get excited that their kids want to come home to their human family but fail to realize that their children are not really home until they are home spiritually. See, a person can become a good member of society, quit an addiction, even visit you for dinner every weekend, and still end up in hell for eternity. When Christian decided he wanted to come home, I was cautiously optimistic but wary. Why? Because he still wasn't ready to surrender to Jesus. I knew from my own life that breaking harmful habits was only a pipe dream without the strength of the Holy Spirit. Our goal as parents is to help our kids into a relationship with Jesus that changes their eternity and their present life. I knew I had to help connect the dots for Christian, just as my father had for me. This took time but now that I had a relationship with my son, I had something to build on.

Even if your child has come home, and you know they have accepted Christ, that doesn't mean their sinful nature is gone. They still have strongholds that the devil helped build that need to be taken down over time, and much growth is needed. When the prodigal returns, we have a mixture of celebration and messiness to contend with.

So the big question is this: When the good season arrives, how do we best care for our prodigals as they return home?

God Can Always Forgive Even When Others Won't

As I (Jim) shared earlier, when I came to believe that Jesus was truly the Son of God, this did not make me feel better, because it just meant that I was going to hell. In my mind there was no way Jesus would forgive me for all I had done. It was my dad who helped me see Jesus for who He truly is. When our child decides that their way of life is killing them, we must help them see the real Jesus. One of the first things we need to reassure our prodigals about is that there's always a way to come back to the Lord. The devil constantly tries to tell prodigals that it can't be done. The devil whispers things like "Don't go home, you're too far away, you've done too many bad things. God doesn't love you anymore." But that's all a lie. The Bible says you can always come home to God through Christ.

How do we know? Just look at a few of the many verses that talk about coming home:

- "Jesus said to them, 'It is not the healthy who need a doctor, but the sick. I have not come to call the righteous, but sinners'" (Mark 2:17). Meaning, Jesus's mission was all about reaching sinful people. Jesus doesn't qualify the sin. Jesus simply cares for sinners. Think of some of the notorious sinners that Jesus reached out to and forgave. There was Zacchaeus, who was a swindler; a prostitute, who washed the Lord's feet; Matthew, who probably with other tax collectors betrayed their country for money and power; the Samaritan woman who had been married five times and was living with another man—not her husband—when she met Jesus; the woman caught in adultery whom the crowd wanted to stone; the thief on the cross; Paul, who had persecuted and murdered Christians; and more.

- "For it is by grace you have been saved, through faith—and this is not from yourselves, it is the gift of God—not by works, so that no one can boast" (Eph. 2:8–9). Meaning, all of salvation is based on grace, on God's gift to humankind, and not on works. The quantity and depth of our sin is not what keeps us from God; it is the essence of sin, the nature of sin in us. The good news of the gospel is that Jesus removes this sin from us by grace through faith. We can always come home to God.

- "If we confess our sins, he is faithful and just to forgive us our sins and to cleanse us from all unrighteousness" (1 John 1:9 ESV). This is a blanket promise of Scripture. Jesus doesn't say that He will remove some sins only, but not all of them. Jesus will forgive us of all our sins. When we repent, Jesus cleanses us from all sins. He removes the sins from our life.

Some prodigals may be deceived into believing that they have committed the only unforgivable sin mentioned in Scripture—blasphemy of the Holy Spirit. The devil convinces them of this—our job is to help them see the true meaning of Scripture.

Some will argue that the Bible describes a sin that leads to death, and that seems to mean some sins can't be forgiven. But that's a wrong interpretation. The passage they're referring to is 1 John 5:16–17:

> If you see any brother or sister commit a sin that does not lead to death, you should pray and God will give them life. I refer to those whose sin does not lead to death. There is a sin that leads to death. I am not saying that you should pray about that. All wrongdoing is sin, and there is sin that does not lead to death.

What is the "sin that leads to death"? This passage is probably describing a person who dies physically without receiving Jesus as Lord and Savior. The person dies in unbelief—that is the sin. For any other sin, we can pray for forgiveness.

But if a person dies while rejecting Jesus, then that sin is "unforgivable."

Keep in mind the context—the apostle John was writing to a church that was concerned about the heresy of Gnosticism. This faulty belief system held that Jesus wasn't God and therefore was not qualified to forgive our sins. If a person held to this heresy, then sin became a troubling issue indeed.

Another legitimate interpretation for this passage is that there sometimes comes a point in the life of a believer who is continuing in stubborn, unrepentant sin, that God may allow physical death. In the early church, this happened to two believers, a husband and wife named Ananias and Sapphira (Acts 5:1–10). They sold a piece of property and gave a portion of the money to the church, but both lied about it, saying they had given the full amount. God took their lives. Most likely, Ananias and Sapphira had a habit of greed and lying, and they seemed to be intent on gaining power. If these two were allowed to get away with their sin, they would have gained important positions within the early church and done great damage. The enemy was seeking to infiltrate the church through people who sought recognition.

Finally, there's another legitimate interpretation. The "sin that leads to death" may be actually talking about separation from other believers, not separation of body and spirit, which is physical death. The overall message of 1 John is a command for us to love one another (1 John 3:11). If people persist in the sin of not loving one another, then this will cause division among people and ultimately lead to a withering of a person's spiritual health. We cannot do our spiritual life alone. We must follow Jesus's commandments to love God and love other people.

The Spiritual Life Is No Place for Lone Wolves

Pastor Perry Noble has spoken publicly about his struggle with alcohol and the restorative break he took from pastoral ministry. It's great to see how he learned from mistakes made along the way. Surely his sin of alcohol abuse led to death—separation from others and God. Note his remarks in the context of our inability to do our spiritual life alone:

> I chose isolation over community. I was a hypocrite—I preached, 'you can't do life alone' and then went out and lived the opposite . . .
>
> Isolation is where self-pity dominated my thinking, thus justifying my abuse of alcohol.
>
> Isolation is where self-doubt dominated my emotions, causing me to believe I just could not carry the weight anymore, and alcohol was necessary for me to make it through another day.
>
> Isolation is where self-hatred dominated my mentality. I literally HATED myself for doing what I was doing, but believed the lie that this was just the way things were and there was no way it could ever get better.
>
> I chose isolation—all the while knowing that a strong community of people who really loved me would rally around me and walk with me through the valley I was in.[1]

Friends, I will continue to drive this message home: we can't do life alone. Spiritual maturity occurs within community when we learn to love God and love others as a body of believers. Maturity includes letting others love you as well. Real relationships with other believers are a necessary part of our lives.

Best Practices When the Prodigal Returns

What does the process of repentance and restoration look like? Again, we look to the story of the prodigal son in Luke 15:11–32.

1. The goal is true biblical spiritual repentance.

We've touched briefly on whether a person needs to hit absolute rock bottom, and the answer is "yes" but also "it depends." Finding the balance is where parenting and loving a prodigal can become quite nuanced and individualized.

Remember, "bottom" for our prodigal is not the goal, as if the overall aim is the lowest point. Rather, the goal is always repentance. Whatever level in the downward spiral a prodigal hits, our hope is that the prodigal will "come to his senses" (Luke 15:17) and turn back to the Lord. Our desire is not that someone will go as low as possible in a behavior, but that they will hit their personal bottom where they'll be jolted into repentance. Sin is a pathway to death if it is unchecked, so we don't want anyone to hit absolute bottom. We want a person to come to the place where they acknowledge they've sinned and need restoration.

How do we know when a turnaround is near? It's when, like the prodigal son, the person's heart is changing. We observe that they begin to search for answers and forgiveness, maybe with the help of someone they can see. It's our job then to probe to see if they are ready to reach out to the One they can't see.

2. We get there one step at a time.

It is important for a prodigal to see the depth of destruction they have caused. This is what happened to the prodigal son: "The son said to him, 'Father, I have sinned against heaven and against you. I am no longer worthy to be called your son'" (Luke 15:21). The son has become aware that he has sinned against both God and his father.

In repenting, a prodigal might initially see that he has harmed either God or a parent. He might first seek to make restitution to one but not both. For instance, a prodigal might be successful in rehab, and this restores his relationship with his parent. But the relationship with God might still be broken. If the relationship with God is not restored, then fellowship is still damaged. A stint in rehab is a step in the right direction, but ultimately, apart from Christ, a person can do nothing (John 15:5).

Remember, the goal is always that a prodigal would repent toward both God and others. A process of rebuilding trust is needed, even after the prodigal has come to the place of confession of sin and a desire for relationship. This trust-building place is kind of a middle ground. During the middle-ground period, Lori and I let Christian come home, but we set boundaries on him at first. For instance, I didn't pay Christian's court debts—he needed to work to pay these off. He had a curfew. He had rules. Only as he was thankful and faithful in little things did I open up the doors to trust.

3. Repentance eventually produces celebration.

There's an overall attitude of rejoicing when a prodigal comes home. The father says to the older brother, "We had to celebrate and be glad, because this brother of yours was dead and is alive again; he was lost and is found" (Luke 15:32). It's so key for us to embrace this attitude, even if we have some mixed feelings.

For instance, we might grieve over what has transpired when the prodigal was away or sorrow at lost opportunities or choices the prodigal has made that led to consequences for them and even for us. Yet we need to place these emotions under the overall umbrella of celebration. The person was lost, but now he is found again. The person was dead, but now she is alive again.

4. Relapses might be part of the process.

The change that occurs in a person's heart as a result of deciding to follow Christ happens in an instant. Yet sanctification is a process, and there are sins that so easily entangle (Heb. 12:1–2). The key for every believer follows in the same Hebrews passage—that we would "run with perseverance the race marked out for us, fixing our eyes on Jesus, the pioneer and perfecter of faith." Why would we need perseverance if problems and sins don't beset us?

Biblically, we do not need to sin. Relapses aren't guaranteed. First John 3:9 says, "No one who is born of God will continue to sin, because God's seed remains in them; they cannot go on sinning, because they have been born of God." This passage refers to sinning habitually or the lifestyle of practicing sin. To understand what it means to practice sin, it helps to think of practicing a sport. You practice because you want to get good at it. God's Word tells us that our heart toward sin is different now. We used to love it and want more and more of it. We practiced it because we wanted to be good at it, but now we love God and hate it when we fail. As true Christians, we will continually seek the face of the Lord and turn from our wicked ways when we notice them. As people who still deal with a sin nature that is in conflict with our new nature, we continually must die to the old nature and "put on the new self" (Col. 3:5–10; Gal. 5:17).

Certainly, the apostle Paul had his share of sinful struggles, even after he became a wholehearted follower of Christ. Paul admitted that he kept doing the things he didn't want to do and had a hard time doing the things he did want to do, and he recognized that sin was still living in him (Rom. 7:19–20).

Complete relapse into addictions or old ways aren't inevitable, yet they are a possibility because our sin nature stands ready to take charge again if we are not diligently abiding in Christ. We all relapse to some extent when we give in to sin big or small. If a prodigal does relapse, we should not think that all is lost. Rather, the process of prayer and restoration occurs again. Grace abounds.

Repentance Doesn't Remove All Consequences of Sin

As noted earlier, repentance means being willing to accept the consequences of wrong behavior—no excuses. When you see your prodigal becoming willing to pay for what they've done, it's a good indication that they are genuinely broken. They are willing to take the punishment and do the hard work to re-earn trust. Often people want to say "sorry" and find all sins forgiven and all privileges restored. This is a surefire way to know that they have no idea how much they hurt others.

When a prodigal comes home, forgiveness can be given but consequences must be dealt with. If your prodigal has just hurt you, then they need to earn back trust. But maybe your prodigal is like mine—he had legal issues to deal with where I had no control.

The prodigal son in Jesus's story understood about consequences. While he was still standing in the middle of the pig farm, first coming to his senses, the son realized that he'd damaged his relationship with both God and his earthly father.

The boy said, "I am no longer worthy to be called your son; make me like one of your hired servants" (Luke 15:18–19). He didn't expect to be returned to his former status as son; he merely hoped to find a place among his father's hired hands.

There were financial consequences to the prodigal's actions. He had used up one-third of the father's estate. We know that the father made it clear to the older brother that all he owned now belonged to the older son. The younger son had no more claim to the father's estate. The father didn't divide the older brother's inheritance and give some to the younger brother. No, the younger brother's inheritance was squandered once and for all. However, with the help of a loving Father and family, it is possible to help prodigals experience restoration in the sense that they can produce a way of life for themselves.

Healing the Family

We've touched briefly on the need to help restore the entire family, not just the prodigal. Let's look at it more closely in the context of Luke 15:11–32. When the older son is out in the field, the good father must help him see the reasons for celebrating a prodigal's return. The older brother doesn't want to do this. In fact, he initially resists the servants. "The older brother became angry and refused to go in."

So the father helped bring restoration between the two separated parties. From the older son's perspective, the younger son had stolen part of his life. Two of my (Jim's) sons also struggled with all that my oldest had taken from us. My younger sons felt they could not confide in me with their struggles because they knew I couldn't handle much more. They felt that our money had gone to rescue my oldest, meaning that there wasn't much for them. They felt so much time had been wasted, and they hated seeing their parents weeping so often. They had each been hurt by their brother as well. Their brother had embarrassed them, and his lifestyle had tainted their reputations. My oldest son had introduced drugs into my youngest's life, and that led him to some poor choices. Both younger sons had desired to spend time with their oldest brother (who was once their hero), only to be disappointed over and over.

Still, part of the father's role is to help reconcile the whole family. The hurt, anger, and bitterness within the other kids can affect their hearts just as rebellion affects the straying one. The devil's favorite poison is unforgiveness, but the heavenly Father desires to bring peace to broken relationships. The father in the Bible story reminded the older son of the wonder of a prodigal's return. He reiterated the amazing truth that all the father owned was at the disposal of the older brother. Ultimately, the father helped the older son gain a vision for the mission of God—that God is in the grace-filled business of loving people and welcoming home sinners.

Lovingly, I had to help my oldest understand the damage he had done so he'd be able to gain a mission to repair brokenness and not just another reason to feel shame. I needed Christian to help me repair the damage of his poor example for Will. I needed Christian to help close the door to drugs in Will's life. Christian did that. He told Will that he needed to listen to Lori and me as parents and that we only wanted to protect him from damage. Christian became an advocate for us, and eventually he became a voice of healing and righteousness in Will's life.

My middle son, Jesse, is more justice-oriented. He felt ignored by his parents and felt that Christian had stolen part of our family life. I mentioned how on a trip to Israel Jesse admitted he felt like the older brother in the story of the prodigal son. Jesse and I talked and prayed through that, and as parents, Lori and I were able to help Jesse forgive Christian, and forgive him more than once. In a family meeting Jesse was able to say to Christian, "I've been like the older brother, and I've judged you. I'm still really hurt, but I'm open to rebuilding a relationship with you."

The point is, sin always has consequences and always seems to hurt those closest to the sinner. But the prodigal may want to return home before the home is healthy enough to make it possible.

Does Returning Home Offer a Blank Slate?

Not long ago I spent time with a young man who had been a prodigal for years but had finally decided to come home. He had been an addict, been in trouble with the law, and deeply hurt those in his family. His legal troubles had started the process of rehabilitation, but what really made the difference was that he found out he was going to be a father. This woke him up, and as time went on, he became a great father to his young child, though he lived hundreds of miles away. When he came to me, he had been sober for two and a half years, had become part of a dynamic church, and served as a youth group volunteer. Then he told me that he was in a major mess. He'd been having severe anxiety for several weeks and sleeping little, so he had asked a friend for one of the friend's anxiety pills to aid sleep. His friend agreed, and the man took the pill and went to bed. The next morning, he woke up, began driving to work, and fell asleep at the wheel. The pills had messed with his system, and he was in an accident. The police arrested him for a DUI.

So he faced a decision. This wasn't even a relapse, technically. But it was illegal to take someone else's prescribed medication. He had tried to go to work, though he was a bit disoriented. He hadn't missed work ever and was proud of showing up on time and being reliable. However, he made a bad choice, and because of his past he got little mercy from the courts. The question was, would those close to him in the church help him? If so, how? Those he was staying with knew that the young man's heart was tender toward the Lord. The man didn't want to return to his former way of life. Overall, he'd made some consistent significant changes. And he felt terrible for this stupid thing he had done—taking medication that wasn't his.

In terms of consequences, that one little mistake grew enormous. His license was suspended for ninety days. His car was wrecked, so he couldn't get to work, which brought on tension with his boss. If he couldn't work, he couldn't pay his bills. If he couldn't pay child support, then he would not be able to see his son, who meant the world to him.

The people he stayed with stepped in to give him a hand up. Church members took turns driving him to work twenty miles away. And he took responsibility too, paying for the gas and working around the house. Slowly he earned enough to get his car fixed. He paid his bail. He faced some tough conversations: with his boss, who needed an explanation, and with his son's mother. That was a talk that terrified him, as he feared losing his right to see his son. He also had to explain to the youth group leaders and even to the kids what he had done and what he was doing to make it right. None of this was easy and it was embarrassing, but he faced it all with the help of Jesus and those in his Life Group. His friends got together and prayed, and God did a work no one expected.

His friends didn't carry the weight of his decisions, but without their help, he would have really fallen hard. I love this story because it shows what can happen when a prodigal meets people who think like the prodigal son's father in Scripture.

What about Boundaries?

I (Bill) am often asked by parents of prodigals what sort of boundaries they should set. One of the best restorative practices I know is for parents to simply resign as "Mommy and Daddy" and take on a new role, that of "Mom and Dad." It's a different dynamic. Parents who act as "Mommy and Daddy" protect a child too much. But parents who act as "Mom and Dad" put the weight of the responsibility back on a child while still giving the child a place of security.

Before the prodigal comes home, they must agree to obey the established rules of the home. If the prodigal does not want to follow these rules and respect these boundaries, then the prodigal will need to find somewhere else to live. In terms of specific boundaries to set, below are some ideas. This can be set up in the form of a contract or even a letter from the parents to the prodigal. (Feel free to adapt these to your own situation.)

Dear _____:

If you stay in our home, then you must respectfully agree to and comply with the following conditions:

1. *You must willingly treat us with respect and speak to us with respect.*
2. *You must willingly keep the established rules of the house.*
3. *You must willingly refrain from profanity, from wearing suggestive clothing, from using tobacco, drugs, and alcohol.*
4. *You must not have friends of the opposite sex in your bedroom.*
5. *You must not have friends in our home in our absence without our permission.*
6. *You must willingly speak to your siblings with respect.*
7. *You must willingly keep an agreed-upon curfew.*
8. *You must willingly partner with us in the work that needs to be done in the home.*
9. *If you are in school, then you must attend school and maintain passing grades.*
10. *If you are not attending school, then you will find and keep a job so you can pay an agreed-upon rent for living in our home.*

We love you. We know the conflict in our home has affected you as much as us. We hope this step on our part will allow us to begin to live in love and peace.

If you choose not to stay in our home, then we hope you know that we love you and that our prayer will be that the distance between us will bring us closer together.

We love you and are waiting for your response.

Mom and Dad

Happy Endings

Bobbi and I (Bill) received a letter from Jim a while back that says it all to us. We really treasure it and share it with you to let you know miracles do happen. When we look at who Jim was as a prodigal for so many years—and the extreme level of tension in the home and how difficult that was for everybody—and then we look at Jim now, how he's following the Lord wholeheartedly, it gives us all cause for hope.

Prodigals can come home!

Here's the letter:

Dear Mom and Dad,

You know that I don't like to be mushy—I never have—but I wanted to write you a letter. I have wanted to for some time, and for one reason or another I haven't found the time. As my son has drifted away from the Lord and from me, it has been the hardest thing in my life. I have come to realize now what I did to you when I was growing up. As I get older, I come to understand how wise you two really were.

I used to say I would never make the mistakes you made as parents, and now I know that it would not have mattered. How foolish I was. I used to think you were weak and that is how I got where I was, but

220

now I know that you were strong and that is how I came back.

Mom and Dad, I want you to know that if you had not been led and empowered by the Lord, then I would have been lost. If you had not stayed strong, I would have broken you and been lost myself.

I want to thank you for all you have done for me. I want to tell you how sorry I am for what I did to you and our family. I was so self-centered, but you showed real love. That is now my only hope for my children.

Dad and Mom, your advice on parenting has been so helpful. You never gave up on me. I know that you two were both used by God to help save me. Again, thank you and forgive me. I don't think I ever really understood what I did to you until this last year. I am so thankful to God for who He gave me as parents.

Dad, I don't want to get mushy about this—don't come up to me and be all touchy feely—just know that my heart is full of love and appreciation for you and Mom. Dad, thanks again for drawing me back, and Mom, thanks for being Dad's stability (along with Jesus).

Jim

10

When the Prodigal Returns to Church

A Tale of Two Churches

A Christian girl went to Bible college and started dating a Christian boy she met there. The boy and the girl quickly grew close and started talking about getting married, but the practical considerations of setting up a household and a life together seemed too large at first. They were both still freshmen, barely eighteen years old. Both sets of parents wanted the kids to get their degrees first before marrying. Preferably jobs too. Marriage was at least four long years off. Maybe more. To the boy and girl, that seemed like far too long to wait.

The couple slipped up one evening. They made one bad choice in their relationship. A week or so later they made another. Then another. Pretty soon they were sleeping together. They weren't "prodigal" in the sense that they were overtly and publicly rebellious. They didn't say they hated God or hated their parents. But they were definitely engaged in immoral behavior, stepping outside God's boundaries for love and commitment in relationships.

A few months passed, and the girl found out she was pregnant. Both the boy and the girl were called into the dean's office at the college. They were open and honest about their sin issues. School administrators asked them to go home for a semester and sort things out. So they did.

The boy went back to his hometown and his church, and the girl went back to her hometown and her church, in another state. Their respective pastors worked with them to help restore their relationships with Christ. Then they worked to help the couple decide how to best move forward. Through counseling, both the boy and the girl decided they weren't truly in love, and a marriage between them would not be the best solution. The girl decided to give the baby up for adoption. Her parents supported her decision. The boy supported the girl's decision, and so did his parents.

Both churches involved in the situation were small churches, each about three hundred members. Both the boy and the girl and their respective families were known in each church. But here's where the story takes a twist.

In the boy's church, he was welcomed and restored.

But in the girl's church, she wasn't.

In the boy's church, his friends surrounded him, prayed for him, and talked him through the experience. A mature spiritual mentor stepped in and discipled the young man. The parents of the young man were surrounded and encouraged and prayed for by their small group.

But in the girl's church, she was met with gossip, isolation, and even contempt. People asked her how she could give up her own baby. Older people in the church made unkind remarks: if she had more sense, she wouldn't have gotten pregnant in the first place. Young women in the college group basically turned their backs on her and didn't invite her to events or into conversations. The girl's parents were all but ostracized. People said the parents must have done something wrong for their daughter to act like that. The pastor tried to remedy the situation, but his voice was scarcely heard, not to the degree where the church climate was changed in any significant way.

More than twenty years have passed. Today, the man is fully walking with the Lord. He's a leader in his church. He's married to a different woman, and they have a family together. He's regularly involved in counseling young people at his church.

But the woman is not walking with the Lord at all. She and her parents didn't stay at her church for long. After she gave up her baby for adoption, she and her parents moved to a different town. Because of their wounds and feelings of rejection, they were afraid to get involved in another church. The woman married a nonbeliever. Today she's divorced and still not walking with the Lord. The parents are still together but nominally Christian at best.

Two churches. Two different responses to returning prodigals. Two different outcomes.

What can we learn?

What Churches That Rescue Sinners Look Like

It surely breaks God's heart when churches are not places of grace and not ready to welcome prodigals when they come home. So many people don't have the Lord to help them in crisis. And effectively, they don't have the Lord's hospital, the church, either.

In a time when family crashes are commonplace and dreams become nightmares, the church becomes more important than ever and often needs to take on the role of an intensive care unit. Besides performing acute care for returned prodigals, the church needs to pay attention to those loved ones who are effectively sitting in the waiting room at the Hospital for Broken Families. They pace the floor while a dear one goes through life-threatening crises. Minutes tick into hours, hours into days, and days into years. Their own faith needs life support while they pace between Satan's accusations and despair.

Sometimes the role of the church is simply to pace by their side. Just to be with them in the waiting, not preaching, not offering ideas for solutions, just understanding. God provided the family of God so we don't have to face our crises alone.

Our churches simply must be prepared to receive back prodigals. Prodigals are coming back to church, and the reception of these prodigals is part of our calling as disciples who follow Jesus. That reception is whole and grace-filled when a church is doing what God calls it to do—loving one another, building relationships, and making disciples who make other disciples.

A church that effectively receives prodigals is made up of people who have experienced forgiveness and don't forget it. When people know that they are forgiven, then they are all the more apt to be forgiving toward other people who are returning home. But if we do not forgive others, then we are like the Pharisees who stood outside of Zacchaeus's house complaining that Jesus was visiting this sinner. If we do not forgive, we have somehow missed the heart of Jesus—that He came to seek and to save the lost. If we do not forgive, then we look at returned prodigals as suspects in crimes rather than prospects with potential for glorifying God.

Many Bible passages remind us we're forgiven. The Lord's Prayer, one of the most well-known sections of Scripture, contains these words of Christ:

> And forgive us our debts, as we also have forgiven our debtors. And lead us not into temptation, but deliver us from the evil one.
>
> For if you forgive other people when they sin against you, your heavenly Father will also forgive you. But if you do not forgive others their sins, your Father will not forgive your sins. (Matt. 6:12–15)

Jesus calls us to continual awareness of our need for forgiveness, and of the forgiveness that's already occurred in our lives. Those statements of Jesus contain strong words. If we don't forgive other people their sins, then God will not forgive our sins. Therefore, we *must* become forgiving people.

Note also the teachings of Jesus from Luke 6:27–38. Even if we have been mistreated by prodigals, our call is still to forgive them. Even if it is hard to love prodigals (particularly when they're not in our immediate family), our call is still to love them. We must remember that they have a heavenly Father who has been waiting for them to return, and they are our brothers or sisters spiritually, if not physically. The greatest thing anyone ever did for me (Jim) was to love my prodigal back in the right direction. The greatest form of worship toward God is to love His lost children back toward home. We are to be merciful as God is merciful. A prodigal might have placed us in a merciless situation, a situation

227

where chaos claimed our lives, but even then we are to show mercy to this person. We aren't to judge or condemn. When a prodigal returns to the Lord, we are to forgive.

> But to you who are listening I say: Love your enemies, do good to those who hate you, bless those who curse you, pray for those who mistreat you. If someone slaps you on one cheek, turn to them the other also. If someone takes your coat, do not withhold your shirt from them. Give to everyone who asks you, and if anyone takes what belongs to you, do not demand it back. Do to others as you would have them do to you.
>
> If you love those who love you, what credit is that to you? Even sinners love those who love them. And if you do good to those who are good to you, what credit is that to you? Even sinners do that. And if you lend to those from whom you expect repayment, what credit is that to you? Even sinners lend to sinners, expecting to be repaid in full.
>
> But love your enemies, do good to them, and lend to them without expecting to get anything back. Then your reward will be great, and you will be children of the Most High, because he is kind to the ungrateful and wicked. Be merciful, just as your Father is merciful.
>
> Do not judge, and you will not be judged. Do not condemn, and you will not be condemned. Forgive, and you will be forgiven. Give, and it will be given to you. A good measure, pressed down, shaken together and running over, will be poured into your lap. For with the measure you use, it will be measured to you. (Luke 6:27–38)

Keep in mind Luke 17:3b–4, where Jesus taught a radical form of forgiveness. We are to forgive people not only once but over and over and over again. Jesus said,

If your brother or sister sins against you, rebuke them; and if they repent, forgive them. Even if they sin against you seven times in a day and seven times come back to you saying "I repent," you must forgive them. (Luke 17:3–4)

Perhaps the strongest command for churches to welcome home prodigals is found in 1 John 4:20, a general command to love:

Whoever claims to love God yet hates a brother or sister is a liar. For whoever does not love their brother and sister, whom they have seen, cannot love God, whom they have not seen.

In other words, if we as churches do not extend love to others, then we cannot claim to love God. That's strong language indeed.

Three Parables for Churches Today

When we think about welcoming prodigals back into our churches, we must remember that the story of the prodigal son is set in the overall context of a larger conversation Jesus had with scribes and Pharisees, the religious people of the day. The religious folks were unhappy with Jesus—and the reason is key to this discussion. Luke 15:1–2 records why they were feeling grumpy:

Now the tax collectors and sinners were all gathering around to hear Jesus. But the Pharisees and the teachers of the law muttered, "This man welcomes sinners and eats with them."

Why were the religious people unhappy? Because Jesus welcomed sinners and even ate with them. Imagine the scenario: Tax collectors had a reputation of being cheaters and liars, mostly known for collecting too much tax from their own people. We don't know exactly what other kinds of sinners were with Jesus, but it's safe to assume they weren't people you'd normally see in church. Yet they had gathered near Jesus to hear Him speak, and Jesus was apparently breaking bread with them. The religious people of the day thought this was scandalous.

Can you see the parallels between this incident in Jesus's life and how churches today treat sinners coming back to church? The question is, does your church have a pharisaical mind-set or a Jesus mind-set? Jesus's way was to welcome prodigals, even before they fully repented. Jesus was all about welcoming people back to God—at any stage of their spiritual journey. That was His mission: to restore people into relationship with their Father.

Even that one small fact—dinner—tells us a lot about Jesus. Jesus was friends with sinners to the point where they felt comfortable enough around Him, not only to listen to what He had to say but to actually invite Him over to their houses for a meal. Ask yourself: What kind of man gets invited to other people's houses to eat? A friendly man, that's who. Jesus wasn't judging the sinners, scorning them, or looking down His nose at them. He wasn't snubbing them or gossiping. The religious people of the day were doing that.

Instead, Jesus sought to befriend sinners. What does a friend do? Jesus relaxed with them and treated them with kindness. Of course He didn't condone their sin or participate in it, but He saw them in light of their need and their potential. He undoubtedly listened to them. He surely laughed with them (after all, how often do sinners hang around with a person who's no fun?). And all the time, Jesus worked to present the gospel to them in words and images and language they could understand.

That's what the three parables that follow in Luke 15 are all about. The scribes and Pharisees were muttering to themselves about what a disgrace Jesus was, wondering aloud why Jesus would ever be friends with spiritual riffraff, but Jesus didn't answer the religious people directly. He went straight into storytelling—and let the stories answer the question.

The first story that Jesus told involves a shepherd who has one hundred sheep. Immediately, with the opening line, all the people listening to Jesus would be able to identify with the story. Shepherds and sheep were a regular part of their lives. Jesus said,

> Suppose one of you has a hundred sheep and loses one of them. Doesn't he leave the ninety-nine in the open country and go after the lost sheep until he finds it? And when he finds it, he joyfully puts it on his shoulders and goes home. Then he calls his friends and neighbors together and says, "Rejoice with me; I have found my lost sheep." I tell you that in the same way there will be more rejoicing in heaven over one sinner who repents than over ninety-nine righteous persons who do not need to repent. (Luke 15:3–7)

When Jesus told this parable, people in the crowd probably murmured and nodded their heads, saying in effect, "Sure, I know how it works to be a shepherd. By all means, if one sheep gets lost, then that becomes the big priority for a shepherd. You need to find that one lost sheep as soon as possible. And when you find it, that's cause for a big celebration."

Jesus followed with a second story, without elaborating on the first. This time, he talked about a woman with ten coins, a story that may have been chosen to speak specifically to women in the crowd. He wanted to engage their lives and hearts too. The shepherd story probably appealed more to the men, because they could readily identify with the job of caring for sheep. The second, a domestic story, appealed more to women of the day. This is what Jesus said:

> Or suppose a woman has ten silver coins and loses one. Doesn't she light a lamp, sweep the house and search carefully until she finds it? And when she finds it, she calls her friends and neighbors together and says, "Rejoice with me; I have found my lost coin." In the same way, I tell you, there is rejoicing in the presence of the angels of God over one sinner who repents. (Luke 15:8–10)

Undoubtedly, every woman in the crowd understood how this story unfolded. The ten coins likely referred to a woman's dowry, the money she would bring into a marriage arrangement. Ten coins was about ten days' wages, indicating she didn't come from a wealthy family.[1] All money would have been extremely precious to that family. So if one of the ten coins was lost, then the woman would have launched an all-out hunt to find it. When the coin was found, everybody—friends, family, and neighbors—would have rejoiced along with her.

Immediately, Jesus launched into His third story, the prodigal son, which we've covered in depth in this book. The point is that Jesus told all three parables to explain why He befriended sinners and tax collectors. He was explaining His mission to reconcile people to the heart of His Father,

God. Jesus was saying that all lost people are important. All lost people are worth going after, finding, and bringing home. All lost people are valuable in the eyes of God. Even sinners. Even tax collectors. Even people the world finds distasteful, disgusting, worthless. Even people you wouldn't find in church.

That's the big attitude shift we need to get across in our churches today. Often the mind-set is that church is only for "us," only for insiders, people who regularly attend. So music choices are made with only insiders in mind. Sermons are preached with only insiders in mind. Programs are designed with only insiders in mind.

But what if we adopted the heart and practice of Jesus and actually befriended and ate with sinners? I know we must be careful here—we must not condone sin and we must not put ourselves into situations that could cause us to fall. But what if the church, meaning Christians who worked together and held each other strong, acted as an invitation-home committee rather than a spiritual security team whose job is to keep the sinners out? What if we adopted the heart of Christ and made our churches into spiritual homes that our prodigals would want to return to? What if we gave prodigals every reason to return home and removed any obstacle that might prevent them from returning?

Then when sinners returned home to God, there would be much rejoicing in our churches!

Turning Hearts toward Christ

The attitude of the good father in Luke 15:20b demonstrates the overall posture churches need to adopt. The verse says, "But while he [the prodigal son] was still a long way off, his father saw him and felt compassion, and ran and embraced him and kissed him" (ESV).

Note that the son was still a long way off when the father saw him. The only way a father could see that far is if he made it a practice of looking a long way down the road. This is a model for our churches to follow—to be constantly waiting, watching, seeking the face of prodigals, longing for their return.

Note that the father left the safety and comfort of his home to go to the son. He actually ran to him. His son was cold, filthy, and had no shoes. It means the father did not wait for the son to clean up or get his life together before the father embraced him.

Notice the father felt compassion for the son. He had already prepared his heart, so he wasn't judgmental or critical. The father's default emotions were compassion, concern, kindness, and love, even though his son had hurt him deeply. How do we develop these default emotions as churches?

It comes down to remembering we are forgiven ourselves, and then constantly praying for the filling of the Holy Spirit in our lives as individuals and as a body of believers. The filling of the Holy Spirit (Eph. 5:18) means our lives are fully yielded to the Holy Spirit, and we are inviting Him to fully control and empower us. We are listening to the Holy Spirit, we are filling our hearts and minds with spiritual matters, we are focused on Christ, and we are growing in grace and in knowledge of the Lord (2 Pet. 3:18). In the words of 1 Thessalonians 5:19, we are not "quenching" the Spirit, or "putting out the Spirit's fire"—meaning we don't want to suffocate the work of the Holy Spirit in our lives.

These things sound like actions that individuals take, but remember that a church is a spiritual body of believers, and we can take corporate actions in this direction too. How often do we pray for our church as a whole, for unity and holiness, for the body's filling and empowering by the Holy Spirit? How often do we pray that our church wouldn't quench the Spirit and that our church would yield itself wholly to God? When corporately, as a body of believers, we have our focus on Jesus, then we are much more able to love other people wholeheartedly, as Christ commands. We are in a much better place to receive prodigals back into our midst. We are looking for their return; we notice when people come back; we listen to their stories, who they are and where they've been and why they're returning. Together we see the prodigals better because there are more eyes looking. Together we are able to give prodigals consistent help, because one person alone is not carrying all the burden. As a church we can share the load.

Just as the good father helped repair the relationship between the older brother and the younger brother, so we are called as churches to this kind of repair work. People are hurt by the actions of prodigals, and our job is to help restore relationships, to be ambassadors of peace and reconciliation. If the prodigals have come from different churches in different towns, then part of our calling is to help connect them with brothers and sisters back home who may have been harmed. How sad it is if one of our prodigals is restored through a different church in a different town and we are not made aware of it. How can we celebrate if we think our lost child is still lost? We need to communicate vital information among churches.

The Role of Confession

Confession is an important key. In recovery ministries at our church, we use a modified version of the Twelve Step program

Bill's Notes for Deeper Reflection
Why Stay in the Church When It Hurts?

Let's face it, the church so often does not live up to these ideals. It falls far short of providing the nurturing environment our prodigals need and feel they can come home to, and sometimes it lashes out in pure meanness. If you've ever been deeply hurt by churches or individual Christians, you are not alone. Even as a pastor, I nearly gave up on the church at 3:30 a.m. one Monday morning, and here are some of the reasons I wrote down:

> Why stay in the church when everything you do is criticized by someone . . . every expression of love is misunderstood . . . you sacrifice money, time, and energy to serve, but others sacrifice nothing . . . you have to be an adult in every situation and you feel like a kid . . . people don't let God help them with their problems but get angry because you don't know how to help them . . . conflict breaks out and battle lines are drawn and no matter what you do, you can't win . . . your words are twisted, and misunderstanding is the norm . . . those who should and could don't, and people who don't know how, or can't, or shouldn't, move into positions of influence. . . .

After writing this and much more of the same, I angrily wrote my resignation from the ministry. The next day I prayed and studied and tore up my resignation, and the following is part of what I wrote:

Why stay in the church and continue to serve?

Because Jesus said directly:

- "If you love Me, keep My commandments" (John 14:15 NASB).

of Alcoholics Anonymous, called Celebrate Recovery. Step 4 is "make a searching and fearless moral inventory of ourselves." Step 7 is "humbly ask God to remove our shortcomings." Step 8 is "make a list of all persons we have harmed, and become willing to make amends to them all." And Step 9 is "make direct

- "Anyone who loves me will obey my teaching. My Father will love them, and we will come to them and make our home with them" (John 14:23).
- "Feed my lambs" (John 21:15).

Because God's Word further says:

- "This is how we know what love is: Jesus Christ laid down his life for us. And we ought to lay down our lives for our brothers and sisters. If anyone has material possessions and sees a brother or sister in need but has no pity on them, how can the love of God be in that person? Dear children, let us not love with words or speech but with actions and in truth" (1 John 3:16–18).
- "But whatever were gains to me I now consider loss for the sake of Christ. What is more, I consider everything a loss because of the surpassing worth of knowing Christ Jesus my Lord, for whose sake I have lost all things. I consider them garbage, that I may gain Christ" (Phil. 3:7–8).
- "Not giving up meeting together, as some are in the habit of doing, but encouraging one another—and all the more as you see the Day approaching" (Heb. 10:25).
- "Let us not become weary in doing good, for at the proper time we will reap a harvest if we do not give up" (Gal. 6:9).

I realized that the Lord has provided for me through His children in His church the help, love, discipling, discipline, and encouragement I've needed. It's my job and privilege to be in a place to pass it on to others.

It can be a helpful exercise to take pen and paper and describe in one paragraph the greatest change that needs to take place in your church so prodigals can be welcomed home.

amends to such people wherever possible, except when to do so would injure them or others."[2] Churches can have a direct role in helping people make moral inventories and amends.

When I (Bill) came back to Christ, I asked the Lord for help and made a list of people I'd harmed who hadn't moved forward, who needed to hear from me. I made amends to all those on that list except one, because I saw such action at that time would only do additional damage. My prayer became, "Lord, would You bring this person face-to-face with me? Would You orchestrate this event so I can say, 'I realize my actions were wrong and selfish. Would you please forgive me?' And please, Lord, let me say this in a way and at a time so that it doesn't bring damage to that person." Sometimes we need to wait many years for such issues to be resolved.

In helping prodigals, we are always seeking to turn hearts toward Christ. Revelation 2:1–7 paints a picture of a church that's working hard for the Lord and persevering under pressure for Christ's sake, but the church has forgotten the most basic principle of loving Christ wholeheartedly. "You have forsaken the love you had at first" (v. 4). When a church holds to that love relationship, it is able to offer the prescription for full restoration to prodigals; that is, they can become connected to the love of God, they can repent of sin, they can find their place personally in the body of Christ. Both church and returning prodigal move in the overall context of Jesus's love.

We are working with a woman who has come back to church after a season of living prodigally. She wants to come back to the Lord, but she's highly embarrassed about what she's done. She's convinced everyone is pointing a finger at her, gossiping behind her back. The devil tells her that nobody is kind or patient or compassionate toward her. But that's a lie. Actually, nobody is holding this woman's actions over her head. Part of her recovery is learning to trust other Christians. She needs to plug back into the family of God. And it's a process to convince her. As a church, we need to help her walk back into fellowship. We need to shut down the "accuser of our brethren" (Rev. 12:10 NKJV) in her life.

Private and Public Confessions

Note in Luke 15:21–22 how the prodigal son confesses to his father:

> And the son said to him, "Father, I have sinned against heaven and before you. I am no longer worthy to be called your son." But the father said to his servants, "Bring quickly the best robe, and put it on him, and put a ring on his hand, and shoes on his feet." (ESV)

The son confesses directly and out loud to his father. That may have been a private confession—or it may have been public, because immediately the father talks to his servants, indicating the servants may have been within earshot of the son's confession. We lean toward the view that the confession was public, even if just because news would likely travel quickly to all in the household. The celebration was certainly public, with all invited.

Clearly the son confesses his sin directly to the one he had harmed, his father, then the son's repentance was made known to all. Sometimes in our churches there are occasions where confessions should be public. If a sin has harmed an entire church body, then the prodigal will want to apologize publicly. Maybe this is done when the prodigal is baptized, as part of an overall testimony. Or perhaps this can be done in a letter.

Confessions do not need to be public if not everybody was wronged. I (Jim) have publicly confessed sin generally (not specifically) in my testimony and even in sermons where it fits. I have shared with my accountability group and others what needed to be shared from both my past and my present.

I'm certainly not proud of what I've done, and honestly, it hurts even to remember some of my past. My testimony is that God can use any idiot—even me. But I don't share every detail of every sin with the entire congregation—and let me stress the importance of this in churches today. Not everybody in a church needs to know everything, and some things are not appropriate to tell anyone in detail. With my congregation I share general matters. With my Life Group, I share more specifically. And with my accountability group of guys, I share the most detailed information that is appropriate. I certainly do not want to cause someone else to sin by sharing my story in a way that glorifies sin or arouses curiosity. I certainly don't want young people to believe it's only those with horrific stories that get a hearing from other believers. I think the best testimonies are those like my son Jesse's. He has walked with Jesus his whole life and avoided so much of the pain that prodigals like me have gone through. Remember that the point in confession isn't to tell prolonged stories of how evil we were. It's to wipe the slate clean before Christ and focus on the goodness, grace, and glory of Jesus in our lives.

Confessions should not be public if the confession would only open a can of worms. In some cases, a confession should not be made even one-on-one. For instance, if you are a man and you have felt lustful thoughts for a woman, we wouldn't counsel you to go to that woman and confess your lustful thoughts. What good would this ever do? Better to confess a sin like this before God, and if needed, with help from your mentor. Get wise counsel about how to refresh and renew your mind.

New Testament writers, in telling their own stories, didn't try to glorify themselves or their sin, nor did they hide their failures. They told the truth. Peter denied Christ. Thomas doubted Jesus. After the death of Christ (prior to the resurrection), all the disciples abandoned the mission of Christ and returned to fishing. They were all willing to say they messed up, but God is good. They messed up, but God can redeem all things. They messed up, but God forgives and restores.

It Ends with Celebration

Bring the best robe. Put a ring on his hand and shoes on his feet. Bring the fattened calf and kill it. Let us eat and celebrate. This is the picture of celebration described in Luke 15:22–23. There's a genuine party going on when prodigals return.

Why party? Because of the good father's words: "For this son of mine was dead and is alive again; he was lost and is found" (Luke 15:24). The reason for celebrating is clear. There is nothing like a happy ending. We celebrate that, although the world has done its best to destroy our prodigals, and us with them, it hasn't won, and a great reconciliation is possible. The whole of the Word of God is a story about relationship regained. That is worth celebrating. It's a celebration for the returning prodigal specifically—and it's a celebration for us all. For we are all in the same boat when it comes to being forgiven by God. God doesn't grade us on a curve. We all have fallen short of the glory of God, and our wages are death. But Christ wipes away the penalty of sin (1 Tim. 1:15), for while we were still sinners, Christ died for us (Rom. 5:8).

We catch a glimpse of this celebration in Ephesians 3:1–21. Paul begins the chapter with a discourse on why he was called to preach to the Gentiles, then he gets so excited he interrupts himself and breaks into a lengthy doxology describing the wonders of Christ's love and forgiveness. He mentions how he was the "least of all the Lord's people" (v. 8a), yet "this grace was given me" (v. 8b). It's as if Paul can't quite contain himself at the thought of "the boundless riches of Christ" (v. 8c) and this idea that "in him and through faith in him we may approach God with freedom and confidence" (v. 12).

Paul is saying that, absolutely, a repentant prodigal is a child of God! Absolutely, a repentant prodigal is forgiven and made free! Absolutely, God isn't finished with repentant prodigals! Absolutely, prodigals are restored and made whole again! Even more, the relationships that God intended them to have with their loved ones can be realized. We can walk through life as family, and that's cause for celebration!

Those truths are what a church needs to impart to a repentant prodigal. A church needs to reassure the repentant prodigal over and over: You are part of a spiritual family. We know you've repented. We will help you repair broken relationships. We will help you make things right. We will encourage you in this new direction you've chosen. We believe that God has good things in store for your life. You are not broken beyond repair. You are not finished in your service to Christ. You are free and forgiven, fully reconciled to the heart of the good Father. You are welcomed home!

11

The Story Isn't Over

I (Jim) described in chapter 4 how I'd been a prodigal and how my dad and mom stayed with me all through that difficult season. They kept praying for me and loving me, even though I gave them a hard time. Then I came to my senses and started studying Christianity. I came back to Jesus and had a few relapses along the way because I initially couldn't get free from the peer relationships that circled around my addiction. Dad and Mom walked me through all that.

I started dating an unbeliever. She was unfaithful to me, and my parents sat me down and said, "Jim, you need to date a believer." So I met a Christian girl and immediately heard their voices in my head saying, "Yes, one like this." I listened and found out they were right. Eventually we married. I carried so much baggage that weighed us down, but Dad and Mom and other Christians walked me through the trials of the relationship. They were there for me and helped me make changes that preserved our relationship and saw it blossom.

I moved to another city and a church there, but I didn't like it. Dad encouraged me to press in instead of backing out. He prompted me to serve, so I started leading the youth group as a volunteer. The four youth in the group eventually became ten and twenty and thirty and fifty. Again, Dad and Mom walked me through that.

Eventually the volunteer position became a full-time job, and I became a youth pastor. My very first board meeting was tragic. The board chairman confessed an affair with his best friend's wife—his best friend was a pastor at the church, and he found out just then, sitting right next to me in shock. After the meeting, I phoned my dad and said, "I'm out of here." But Dad told me to stay. He told me that right now the church would need me more than ever and that heroes are made in wartime, not peacetime. So I stayed. Later I had run-ins with the pastor and discovered that he wasn't the kind of leader I wanted to follow. Again I called my father, ready to leave. He said, "Why do you think God moved David from the sheep pen to function under King Saul, when Saul was so messed up?" I had no idea. He said, "Because God wanted to show David what it was like when a person rebels. God wanted David to learn what not to do when he became king. You can learn much from a poor leader if you're paying attention. Don't run from the hard lessons and trials that come from ministry. Don't run from the battlefield. Be part of the solution." So I stayed. Again, Dad and Mom and a growing number of Christians walked me all through that.

As I learned and grew, the size of the youth group grew as well. This led to another crises as the size of the youth group eclipsed the size of the adult church. The older church people felt that they were losing their church. The youth were becoming a nuisance to them and strangers began attending. These new people had ideas and objections and needs, and they wanted to go in a different direction than the old guard had set. Because many of them were new Christians, they didn't understand why things were done the way they were. They also came with problems (most new believers do). A war was brewing. I faced choices: constantly fight with the old guard, or accept what they wanted and live in that box. I could lead the people in a new direction, but they seemed fearful. Some whispered in my ear that we should just move across town and start a new church.

I called my dad and I will never forget what he said. He told me, "Jim, the church belongs to God, and you have no right to split His church." He said, "There is a big difference between a split and a church plant. A church plant doesn't divide people. It starts with a new group with the blessing of an established church. These whisperers are being used by the enemy to draw you into rebellion against your leaders." So the question was, do I stay and submit until the Lord opens a door for change, or do I request the elders' help to plant a church in a new and needy area?

That's when Aaron Couch and I, with a couple of committed families, started Real Life Ministries, with the blessing of our established church as well as the partnership of a couple of others. We used the principles I'd practiced earlier in the wrestling team and youth group. Using Life Groups, we began to disciple people from the ground up and intentionally help them grow in the faith. In my own life, what had made the most difference was my father and mother with a Bible in their hands. In other words, intentional relationship with mature believers had meant everything to me. It was clear this had been Jesus's method with His disciples. I had a lot of conversations with my mom and dad along the way. This journey with my parents and other friends and coworkers is at the source of all the books I have written—*Church Is a Team Sport*, *Real Life Discipleship*, *The Real Life Discipleship Manual*, *Disciple-Shift*, *The Power of Together* and its workbook, and now this book.

Here's my point: *I was helped along the way to grow to maturity*. That fact is key. When I was a prodigal, my parents helped me return home to the Lord, yes, but then they stayed with me. They kept discipling me all the way through the various seasons of life where I grew in my faith, developed real relationships with people, began to serve, and eventually became a mature disciple of Jesus who makes other disciples. My mom and dad discipled me all the way to spiritual maturity, helped me find my place in the body of Christ, and then encouraged me to use my skill set and gifts for the glory of God.

That's our calling as individual followers of Jesus and as churches. Our job is not simply to help prodigals repent so they can lead a sanitized, publicly acceptable life. Our job is to disciple people until they are wholehearted disciples of Jesus, in deep relationships with God and other people, and until they are functioning in service in the body of Christ. That's spiritual maturity.

We've talked about a lot of different ideas in this book. Now let's grab this one final thought: the story isn't over. There's still work to be done after the prodigal returns—the work of ongoing discipleship.

How Quickly They Can Slip Away

Israel was led by God through the wilderness to the banks of the Jordan River, preparing to go into the Promised Land. Twelve spies were sent into the land to see what it was like. Ten spies came back and said that the land was exceedingly good, but there were giants in the land, giants who could not be defeated. Israel couldn't do it, they said. Those ten spies swayed Israel into staying put.

But two of the spies, Joshua and Caleb, reminded the people that God was leading them, God was fighting for them, and God had already given them the land. It didn't matter if there were giants in the land, those giants could be defeated. Joshua and Caleb were the only two, with their leader Moses, who had faith that God would do what He said.

God told the Israelites that as a result of their disobedience, they must turn away from the Promised Land and go back into the wilderness for forty years. The older generation would die off, and a new generation rise up. Only the new generation would go into the land. Eventually Moses died, and Joshua became leader of the new generation. They entered the land. Joshua led the Israelites in the defeat of the city of Jericho, then in taking most of the Promised Land.

Toward the end of the book of Joshua, we learn this:

After these things, Joshua son of Nun, the servant of the LORD, died at the age of a hundred and ten. And they buried him in the land of his inheritance, at Timnath Serah in the hill country of Ephraim, north of Mount Gaash.

Israel served the LORD throughout the lifetime of Joshua and of the elders who outlived him and who had experienced everything the LORD had done for Israel. (24:29–31)

That's a good report. During the time of Joshua, the whole nation followed the Lord and continued to follow the Lord while the elders who outlived Joshua were still living.

But not long afterward, as the book of Judges begins, the story continues and it's not so good:

> After that whole generation [Joshua's] had been gathered to their ancestors, another generation grew up who knew neither the LORD nor what he had done for Israel. Then the Israelites did evil in the eyes of the LORD and served the Baals. They forsook the LORD, the God of their ancestors, who had brought them out of Egypt. They followed and worshiped various gods of the peoples around them. They aroused the LORD's anger because they forsook him and served Baal and the Ashtoreths.
>
> In his anger against Israel the LORD gave them into the hands of raiders who plundered them. He sold them into the hands of their enemies all around, whom they were no longer able to resist. Whenever Israel went out to fight, the hand of the LORD was against them to defeat them, just as he had sworn to them. They were in great distress. (2:10–15)

So, here's what we want you to see in those two passages. In the time span of only one generation, an entire nation goes from serving the Lord to turning their back on Him and worshiping idols. *Bam!* It happened that fast. When the people had a good leader—Joshua—they followed the Lord. But another generation grew up who forgot what God had done for Israel, refused to know God, and turned to idol worship. Because of that, all sorts of calamity came upon Israel, and they were in big trouble.

Joshua had done a great job of ministering to and leading the people politically. But he and his leaders failed to reach their own children. This is the lesson for us. The process of discipleship must enter our homes and churches. We must not only reach today's prodigals with the message that they can come home, but just as importantly, we must do all we can to keep our children from leaving in the first place.

Reaching the Next Generation

How do we do this? How do we disciple people now and care for the strays now, while also reaching the next generation? The answer is, we need a reproducing type of discipleship. We need to be disciples who make other disciples, and so on and so on. As parents we must love the Lord wholeheartedly and then impress a knowledge of God on our children. We need to focus on talking about Jesus as we sit, walk, lie down, and go about daily life, according to Deuteronomy 6:4–9. Rather than focusing on worldly success, we must get our children ready for eternal success.

We hear so many stories of parents who raise their children with a smattering of Christianity and a huge focus on the idols of sports or education or entertainment, then the children turn away from God in college years to profligate living and unsound thinking. The family schedule had been dictated by the sports schedule and the drive for scholarships, with any free time filled by entertainment. The children's spiritual education had been reduced to maybe praying before meals. There had been no time for church activities, Christian friends, Bible study, or deep conversations about eternal truth. This is not a picture of raising children in the Lord.

So what is the answer? We have been given three wonderful gifts—the Word of God, the Spirit of God, and the people of God—to help us in this battle. If we don't use these gifts and get our kids ready to grasp and use these gifts, then we are just handing them over to the enemy. Our strategy for raising children to follow Jesus or winning back prodigals must be multifaceted and center on these three big components working together. Too many churches and families focus on only one or two of the three rather than all. We need them all.

1. It takes the Word of the Lord.

The question is, how do we make disciples who not only survive but thrive in a war-torn prodigal world? How do we raise children to be disciples who are able to make other disciples? The Word of God must become our guide and our source of light and direction. We must read the Bible, teach the Bible, memorize the Bible, and pass the Bible along to the next generation. We must do this in such a way that our kids can apply it to their lives. They must understand not only the rules but the reason behind the rules—God's love. Our goal is not simply to engage with Scripture, but to know the God of Scripture. We and our children don't merely need to know about God; we need to know God in personal relationship.

A Barna poll showed that only 7 percent of American adults chose "Bible reading" as their most fulfilling spiritual activity. Barna wrote, "The findings of this research . . . have shown that most Americans are ill-schooled in the content of the Bible; they do not believe they have experienced the presence of God in the past year, and less than one out of every five churched adults has any process or system designed for spiritual accountability."[1]

So when it comes to being reproducing disciples, we must be in the Word of God ourselves, then teach our children to be in the Word of God. We must train up godly leaders who help the next generation love the Word of God and encounter God through it.

So many passages of Scripture point to this. Here are just a few:

> This Book of the Law shall not depart from your mouth, but you shall meditate on it day and night, so that you may be careful to do according to all that is written in it. For then you will make your way prosperous, and then you will have good success. (Josh. 1:8 ESV)

According to this passage in Joshua, we are to think about the Word and put into practice carefully everything it says.

> Blessed is the man
> who walks not in the counsel of the wicked,
> nor stands in the way of sinners,
> nor sits in the seat of scoffers;
> but his delight is in the law of the Lord,
> and on his law he meditates day and night.
>
> He is like a tree
> planted by streams of water
> that yields its fruit in its season,
> and its leaf does not wither.
> In all that he does, he prospers. (Ps. 1:1–3 ESV)

According to this psalm, we are to enjoy the Word of God and think about it day and night. The Word of God keeps us grounded. When the storms of life hit, God's Word keeps us standing and growing.

Man shall not live by bread alone, but by every word that comes from the mouth of God. (Matt. 4:4)

These words came directly from Jesus. He clearly put great value on meditating, memorizing, and metabolizing God's Word. When Jesus was tempted by the devil in the wilderness, He responded by relying on promises in Scripture.

So Jesus said to the Jews who had believed him, "If you abide in my word, you are truly my disciples, and you will know the truth, and the truth will set you free." (John 8:31–32 ESV)

As disciples of Jesus, our call is to "abide" in Christ through the Word of God. That's how we know we are truly disciples, and we experience how God's Word sets us free.

Of course, because God's Word is so life-producing and so important, the world attacks it. The world says scientists and scholars have proven the Bible false and full of contradictions. Our children face this and need good answers as they head off into a culture that is resolute about destroying their faith.

As a parent, have you accepted your role as chief architect of getting them ready? Some want the church to do it all, so they put their kids in youth group and Sunday school or a Christian school. This is all important, but you are the one who must orchestrate all of this. The church is there to support you, but you hold the God-given responsibility. It's awesome to watch a parent smile as their kid serves the Lord. It's amazing to watch a proud grandparent stand at the godly wedding of their grandchild. It's also heartbreaking to see parents or grandparents who did not do their job and then suffer through the agony that their kids bring on. I am not saying that the failure of a child to walk with Jesus is always the parents' fault. As we have written, every child must make their own choices, but we need to do our part to help them make right choices. You may protest that you've never been discipled and don't know how to do your part. I would say it's your job to figure it out rather than make excuses. Be in a church with good support. Go to a Christian who is training their kids right and ask them to show you how. Read the great wealth of books on Christian child-raising. Be humble and coachable. Make it your mission in life to be the person God calls you to be as a parent.

2. It takes the Spirit of God.

Do we want to become disciples who make other disciples? Along with the Word of God, it takes the Spirit of God. Paul in Romans 8:14 says, "For those who are led by the Spirit of God are the children of God."

The Holy Spirit isn't an "it" or a "force" or an impersonal being. The Holy Spirit is a Person, the third member of the Trinity. How do we know this? Because Jesus described the Holy Spirit this way. The Holy Spirit lives in us. The Holy Spirit is our advocate—One who supports us and champions our spiritual growth. The Holy Spirit brings to mind Scripture to apply to our lives. Jesus told His disciples,

> I will ask the Father, and he will give you another advocate to help you and be with you forever—the Spirit of truth. The world cannot accept him, because it neither sees him nor knows him. But you know him, for he lives with you and will be in you. . . . *All this I have spoken while still with you. But the Advocate, the Holy Spirit, whom the Father will send in my name, will teach you all things and will remind*

253

you of everything I have said to you. (John 14:16–17, 25–26, emphasis added).

The Holy Spirit will work continually to transform our minds and hearts and lives if we allow Him, and He gives us power to change. The Holy Spirit applies the Word of God to the people of God. He fuels the life-transforming ministry described in Romans 12:1–2:

> Therefore, I urge you, brothers and sisters, in view of God's mercy, to offer your bodies as a living sacrifice, holy and pleasing to God—this is your true and proper worship. Do not conform to the pattern of this world, but be transformed by the renewing of your mind. Then you will be able to test and approve what God's will is—his good, pleasing and perfect will.

None of us can overcome our prodigal tendencies apart from the Spirit of God. We don't have the power to transform our lives ourselves. Not fully. We cannot overcome sin without the power of God. Romans 8:26–27 says,

> In the same way, the Spirit helps us in our weakness. We do not know what we ought to pray for, but the Spirit himself intercedes for us through wordless groans. And he who searches our hearts knows the mind of the Spirit, because the Spirit intercedes for God's people in accordance with the will of God.

That means that the Holy Spirit is at work within us even when we don't know what we need to pray for. As parents, if we have prodigal children, we may have so much tension and distress in our lives that it becomes difficult to pray. All we can do is cry out to the Lord, "Help." The Holy Spirit of God knows that what we are really praying is more like, "Restore us. Protect us. Transform us. Renew us." The Holy Spirit intercedes for us with God the Father and translates our groans to God.

So as we take in the Word of God, the Holy Spirit empowers us not only to remember it but to live it. The Word of God and the Spirit of God work together in us, but there is one more gift the Lord has given to us—people!

3. It takes the people of God.

If our aim is to be disciples who make other disciples, then we cannot depend on the Bible and the Spirit only. God also uses people to teach, support, correct, and encourage us. This might sound heretical to some Christians, particularly Protestants who hold to the doctrine of *sola scriptura*—that the Bible is the only authority that guides our spiritual lives. And while the Bible certainly is the only absolute authority, the Bible itself teaches us the concept that Christians need other Christians. Jesus Himself told us to go and make disciples, to baptize and teach. Paul tells us to train up reliable men who are able to teach. The family of God is to be a loving community who passes on the faith by teaching men and women to accurately handle the Word of God. We are the body of Christ, held together and directed by Christ our head. We need the people of God to help us grow to spiritual maturity. Let's look at several passages that teach this.

Ephesians 2:19–20 says, "You are no longer foreigners and strangers, but fellow citizens with God's people and also members of his household, built on the foundation of the apostles and prophets, with Christ Jesus himself as the chief cornerstone." This means we are part of the Lord's family. God designed us for relationships with one another.

First Peter 3:8 tells us to "be like-minded, be sympathetic, love one another, be compassionate and humble." How we act toward one another reveals our spiritual maturity. If we do not love one another, we may be knowledgeable and gifted, even obedient, but not mature. We might know the Bible inside and out, but if we don't apply the Bible's teaching and love one another deeply, from the heart, then all our knowledge isn't worth anything.

First John 1:7 says, "If we walk in the light, as he is in the light, we have fellowship with one another, and the blood of Jesus, his Son, purifies us from all sin."

Hebrews 3:12 says, "See to it, brothers and sisters, that none of you has a sinful, unbelieving heart that turns away from the living God. But encourage one another daily, as long as it is called 'Today,' so that none of you may be hardened by sin's deceitfulness."

Fellowship with one another is absolutely needed. Christians sometimes get into this harmful way of living where they separate themselves from other believers and isolate themselves from the church. They may attend services, and even serve in church, but they are not developing real relationships with other people, knowing and being known.

Hebrews 3:12 makes it clear that the way we stop our hearts from becoming hardened is through relationships. We are to encourage one another. That word *encourage* means to inspire, to spur on, as we normally define it, but it also means to admonish, to confront in love. And we are to encourage one another daily. We need to be reminded who we are daily, and we get this through our brothers and sisters in Christ. Life is meant to be lived together. All the fruit of the Spirit is relational by nature.

God gives us His Word as a manual for life. He then gives us the power source for living that life—His Spirit. He then gives us His people to help us when we fall and to encourage us when we do it right. We can do the mission the Lord has given us when we work together. The church is God's plan A and there is no plan B.

Prodigals Do Come Home

What do you do if you love someone who's a prodigal? You keep hoping. Keep praying. Keep preparing your home and church to be places that prodigals want to come home to. You get or stay connected with other believers so that you can experience all that God has for you. By doing this, you show your prodigal that life can look different than the life they are living. You experience abundant life, live according to the Lord's design, and keep strong. This is all attractive. You are on the rock and can pull them out of their stormy ocean when they will let you. You keep ministering in the meantime. You keep going forward in love.

And prodigals do come home. Not always. There is no guarantee. But it does happen. We ourselves are prime examples of that. I (Bill) didn't just need a doctor or a hospital, I needed a miracle. In the middle of our crazy period, I took a look in the mirror at myself and saw a husband, dad, and pastor looking back at me. I realized I had all the qualifications for those roles but failed to have the one qualification needed for leadership: no one was following me.

I gave my family good orders, I preached good sermons, I read good books and did the things I'd seen other successful people doing, but my home and church were in crises that I didn't know how to deal with. People were listening to my words, but they were not following my steps. Even worse, my own children were not following me.

I started looking for someone or something else to blame, thinking:

- It must be my family's fault. I'll change them.
- It must be my church's fault. I'll change churches.
- These must be the wrong helps. I'll find a better book or counselor.
- If only I could get my child to a counselor, we could be a happy family.
- If only I had been older when we had children.
- If only my wife could stay home with the children instead of working outside the home.
- If only I could afford to keep the children in Christian school.

If only, if only, if only—I thought of them all.

I finally came to understand that I needed God to take me—a broken-down, poor excuse for a husband, dad, and pastor—and make me a miracle. I can look back now and realize that I needed to learn to turn my life over to the Lord so He could begin making my mess into a miracle. Until those in my world could see Him changing me, no church or counselor, no amount of hard work, no book or class, not even a two-parent home or a Christian school could bring about the changes needed. My children didn't need me to be a better parent, they needed me to become a transparent one so they could see the Lord at work within me. They needed to see God changing me and gain the hope that He could change them too.

You see, we must first be a living advertisement of what Jesus Christ can do. This does not mean that you are a completed work of God, but you are a miracle in the making.

When I started breaking the habit of trying to change everyone else in my world and started allowing the Lord to work in me, real change began to occur. God began to work first in my own life. Then my wonderful godly wife had a partner to work with in the marriage and in the home. It was then, in the midst of the crisis in my home, in spite of our brokenness, that people started listening to my sermons and following my example. They didn't follow me because I was right. They followed me because they could see God at work in my life.

Here's how I learned the secret to becoming a miracle in the making. I don't know about you, but sometimes I read the Bible and it's like eating cornflakes without milk. Other times, when my heart is ready, it's like a feast and the Scripture transforms me. One day I was reading Luke 4:18–21, where Jesus enters the temple, picks up the Scriptures, reads a portion, then closes the book, returns it to the attendant, and sits down. The eyes of everyone in the synagogue are on Him, and He says, "Today this Scripture is fulfilled in your hearing."

I was intrigued and wanted to know more, so I looked at Isaiah 61, which Luke was quoting and Jesus was reading.

The Spirit of the Sovereign LORD is on me, because the LORD has anointed me to preach good news to the poor. He has sent me to bind up the brokenhearted, to proclaim freedom for the captives and release from darkness for the prisoners, to proclaim the year of the LORD's favor and the day of vengeance of our God, to comfort all who mourn and provide for those who grieve in Zion—to bestow on them a crown of beauty instead of ashes, the oil of joy instead of mourning, and a garment of praise instead of a spirit of despair. They will be called oaks of righteousness, a planting of the LORD for the display of his splendor. They will rebuild the ancient ruins and restore the places long devastated; they will renew the ruined cities that have been devastated for generations. . . . And you will be called priests of the LORD, you will be named ministers of our God. (vv. 1–4, 6)

When I read this passage, I knew it was not only for ancient people but for me and my family. This Scripture could be fulfilled in us.

I discovered that He can indeed bring good news to the afflicted, because He brought it to me. He can bind up the brokenhearted, because He bound up my heart. He can set the captive free, because He set my filthy life and mind free. I discovered too that He could make this a favorable year; He could comfort my mourning soul; He could place praise into my failing heart; He could cause me to stand like a giant oak tree in the storms of life, bring praise to Himself from my life, and allow me to rebuild the ruins and take away the devastations; and—miracle of miracles—He would allow me to be called a priest of the Lord.

On the days when I focus on the facts that "He can, He could, He would, and He did," I have the key to being a joy-filled contented man. As the Lord began to make miracles of us as individuals and then as a married couple, we began to watch God reach out to reclaim our family one at a time. When I found out that He would and could do these things for me, He gave me hope for my marriage, my children, and my church.

Luke 19:10 says, "The Son of Man has come to seek and to save that which was lost" (NASB). It does not say that He came to restore what man had lost, that is, his health, wealth, and happiness. He came to restore lost man himself. He came to make us a miracle.

Since the only one you can make decisions for is you, ask the Lord to help you get your eyes off your mate and your children and on yourself. You are responsible for yourself, to take your broken heart to the Lord and allow Him to begin, moment by moment, day by day, week by week, to help you rebuild your life and family. I could once be best described as a "sheep without a shepherd," and now I'm a miracle in the making. I recommend that you take your broken heart and dreams to the Lord and let Him begin to make a miracle of you.

The Final Call to Love

When sin entered the world in the Garden of Eden, all human relationships were broken. We inherit that brokenness at birth, and it troubles us throughout life. The devil told Eve a half-truth when he said eating the fruit wouldn't lead to death. It didn't lead immediately to physical death, but it did cause immediate relational death, and it set in motion the process of physical death. God knew what He was talking about.

We are like phones that stay charged as long as we are connected to the outlet (God), but once separation between the phone charger and the wall occurs, we begin to run off our own battery. We run off our own understanding, which is limited to our own thoughts, feelings, and desires. And our battery slowly dies.

Some ask why God would allow the world to continue once it was contaminated. In answer, Jesus told the parable of the prodigal son, revealing God's overall plan to save us. God has done what Jesus describes in the story. God has allowed us to go into a world of our making so that we could discover that all of it leads to pig slop. He did this because He is a God of relationships, and relationships require choices. God chooses us, but we must choose Him too. God allows us to go off to a far country and squander the wealth He has given us. He allows this, yet waits for us to return home. He longs to restore relationship. In fact, even before we think about returning, He orchestrates events to draw us back. He doesn't cause sin, but He allows it in hopes that as we experience sin's brokenness, we will decide that God the Father was right all along—we will come to our senses and go home. When He glimpses us coming, He runs to us.

Those of us who stay home can still miss the heart of God. The older brother was furious with his father because the father didn't give his sibling what the older brother thought the younger deserved. The older brother felt he had been his father's slave, even though all he owned came from a generous father. The older brother lacked love for his sibling. Notice that the father's heart was to get the older son to come into the house and celebrate with the family, including the younger son. The father wanted the two brothers in relationship with each other.

Likewise, our God wants to restore our relationships with Him through what He has done in Christ, and He also wants to restore our relationships with one another.

That's what this entire book has been about—the love of God for us, the love of God that flows through us and that we extend to other people. And that's the big encouragement that we want to leave you with as we close this book: the hope of love. Prodigals do come home. Lives do change. God can make all things new again. And in the meantime, our call always is to love. If you love someone, and they know those relational ropes are there, then that love and those relationships will help a person turn again to Christ.

Our call is to love continually. To never stop loving.

NOTES

Chapter 1 Broken Families, Broken Churches

1. "America's Changing Religious Landscape," Pew Research Center, May 12, 2015, http://www.pewforum.org/2015/05/12/americas-changing-religious-landscape/.

2. Sarah Pulliam Bailey, "Christianity Faces Sharp Decline as Americans Are Becoming Even Less Affiliated with Religion," *Washington Post*, May 12, 2015, https://www.washingtonpost.com/news/acts-of-faith/wp/2015/05/12/christianity-faces-sharp-decline-as-americans-are-becoming-even-less-affiliated-with-religion/?tid=a_inl.

3. Ed Stetzer, "Dropouts and Disciples: How Many Students Are Really Leaving the Church," *Christianity Today*, May 14, 2014, http://www.christianitytoday.com/edstetzer/2014/may/dropouts-and-disciples-how-many-students-are-really-leaving.html.

4. Ibid.

Chapter 2 Building a Home That's Hard to Leave

1. John Piper, "How Christ Fulfilled and Ended the Old Testament Regime," Desiring God, February 23, 2005, http://www.desiringgod.org/articles/how-christ-fulfilled-and-ended-the-old-testament-regime.

Chapter 5 The Pain of Exposure

1. Joseph M. Scriven, "What a Friend We Have in Jesus," 1855, public domain.

Chapter 9 When the Prodigal Returns Home

1. Perry Noble, "Perry Noble on the Roots of His Alcohol Abuse: 'I Was a Hypocrite,'" *Relevant*, October 19, 2016, http://www.relevantmagazine .com/slices/perry-noble-roots-his-alcohol-abuse-i-was-hypocrite.

Chapter 10 When the Prodigal Returns to Church

1. Craig S. Keener, *IVP Bible Background Commentary, New Testament* (Downers Grove, IL: InterVarsity Press, 1993), 232.
2. http://12step.org/.

Chapter 11 The Story Isn't Over

1. The Barna Group, "Americans Describe Sources of Spiritual Fulfillment and Frustration," Ventura, CA, November 29, 2004.

ABOUT THE AUTHORS

Jim Putman is the founder and senior pastor of Real Life Ministries in Post Falls, Idaho, one of the most influential churches in America. He is the author of *Church Is a Team Sport*, *Real Life Discipleship*, *DiscipleShift*, and *The Power of Together*, as well as the widely adopted Real Life Discipleship program.

Bill Putman has served in ministry for more than fifty-two years as a pastor, church planter, and executive pastor. He currently serves at Real Life Ministries in leadership development and follow-up ministries. He is the author of *Daddy, I'm Pregnant* and *Life Sure Is Confusing* and the developer of the GODISNOWHERE app that helps people build up their faith.

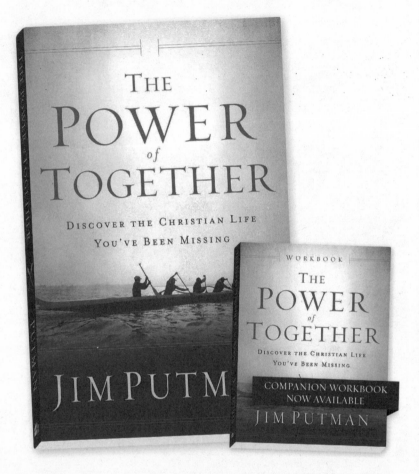

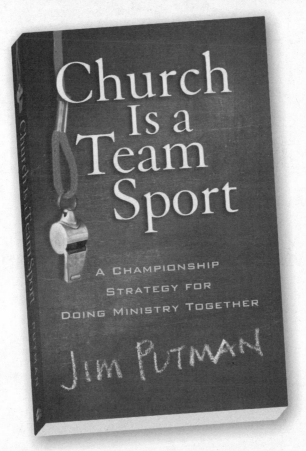